ANTHROPOLOGY OF DISASTER MANAGEMENT

ANTHROPOLOGY
OF
DISASTER MANAGEMENT

Edited
by
SACHINDRA NARAYAN

GYAN PUBLISHING HOUSE
NEW DELHI-110002

ANTHROPOLOGY OF DISASTER MANAGEMENT

(Anthropology, Industry, Management, Sociology)

ISBN : 81-212-0683-9

Published in 2000 in India by
Gyan Publishing House
5, Ansari Road, Darya Ganj
New Delhi - 110002

Laser Typeset at A.S. Printers, Delhi

Printed at Mehra Offset Printers

Contents

Contents

Preface

The 14th International Congress of Anthropological and Ethnological Sciences was held from 26 July to 1 August, 1998 at Williamsburg, Virginia, USA. The last in this century. The theme of this conference, which was held at the College of William and Mary was 'The 21st Century: The Century of Anthropology'. The Williamsburg conference had three specific objectives: (i) to reflect on the accomplishments and lessons of the past 100 years of anthropology; (ii) to examine the challenges of anthropology in the new millennium; and (iii) to explore the application of insights of anthropology to public policy, education, business and human services.

Anthropologists are aware that there are many anthropological "realities" produced and reproduced in local and global systems of thought and knowledge. This awareness encourages us to classify the issues we confront in light of the insights we have gained as anthropologists since the Torres strait expedition of 1898. During the scientific session of the Congress it was discussed that it was necessary for Anthropology, the Science of Man in its totality to deal with disaster management towards the close of this century while we equip ourselves for the 21st century with management skills.

In tribal India, and also in other parts of the world, we frequently find drought, flood, epidemic and mysterious diseases leading to depopulation, migration and other allied problems. Being tribals they are unable to draw immediate attention of the policy makers, concerned governments, activists, anthropologists, etc. Ethnographic studies and the applied anthropology fail to cater to the needs of the tribals.

Therefore, the Anthropology of disaster management becomes a necessary dimension of Anthropology of the 21st century.

According to one estimate about 5,200 disasters took place in 178 countries between 1963 and 1992 causing on an average 100 deaths.

Mankind has survived and lived with natural disasters right from the days of the mythical universal deluge. Floods, volcanic eruptions and earthquakes have plagued and devastated humanity since time immemorial. Recurring floods are believed to have contributed, among other factors, to the extinction of the flourishing Indus valley civilisation of South Asia in ancient times. You can do nothing about shifting of tectonic plates beneath the oceans causing devastating earthquakes or lava simmering underneath the earth's crust from erupting violently. And if our astronomers are to be believed, our planet is facing the dire prospect of total annihilation by a Hailey's comet, striking it in less than one and a quarter century from now. The exact year of their dark predication is 2116. Human endeavour in respect of such natural disasters, which are beyond human control and regulation is limited to deep study, fact finding and forewarning by natural scientists concerned.

The famines in Bihar in the late 18th century have been discussed along with concentration on 'Governance of Disaster: Its Management' Disaster is a calamity which is suddenly thrust either by nature or by man himself on himself. It blows out, dismantles and smashes all the 'orders of life' haywire. It may occur in any walk of life and at any moment of time. It has a potentiality of putting a man non-plussed. It obviously causes immense loss to mankind. In the 20th century, if anything has browbeaten mankind quite often it is 'disaster'—disaster of every kind. The more the mankind has progressed and developed, the more it has become vulnerable to the blows of disaster. Disaster keeps on striking in all parts of the world, with almost a 'disciplined regularity'. It may be a sudden outbreak of war at one place, or it may be an earthquake at some other place. It may be flood, hurricane, nuclear leakage at some place, or it may be a big fire suddenly flashing and flaming in blocks of apartment at some other place. One may think of any misfortune which suddenly hits human population. And it all has a 'disaster' potential.

But then how to meet the challenges of disaster? It is going to be a towering exercise for the man of the 21st century. To meet the challenges of disaster, we need to evolve some 'universal' and some 'specific' tools which may effectively handle the situation of disaster. Unless we do that, we shall not be able to save the world from great catastrophes to which mankind now seems more vulnerable to, in the years to come. Obviously, the disaster management is going to be a vital discipline of study in the 21st century.

The 'style', the 'technique', the 'policies', the 'implementation' and 'execution' of policies related to disaster management and governance have quite often in past triggered off several incidents of disaster. The governments all over the world have at times initiated such policies which invariably led to a chain of great catastrophes in their respective countries. The nature of such policy implementation in different countries have been quite diverse. From 'apartheid' to 'social justice'—their implementations and executions have sordidly resulted into great social clashes, counter-clashes and even upheavals of great magnitude. Even the developmental policy executions have sometimes resulted into great protests and rebellions by people in several countries. We may, for example, see the questions of policy implementation in the field of 'environmental pollution', 'ecological sustenance', etc. However, such cases of policy implementations cannot always be attributed to defective policy formulations at the topmost level. Sometimes, even good and socially imperative policies, when implemented or executed, have resulted into disastrous consequences.

Of all the peace time professions, the underground coal mining is by far the most hazardous one. There have been disasters in coal mines in every coal producing country of the world. Despite good safety records every mine must prepare for prevention of disaster and meeting any emergency. Every one who has a role to play in emergency must be clear about his role so that there is no confusion when any emergency arises. There should be frequent interaction with state administration for maintaining law and order at the time of emergencies.

The chapter on 'Ethnicity-Policy-Gap-Problem Management' highlights the nature of disasters of coal mines and has elaborated that the management problems of the coal mines can be minimized in case the model of sharing of revenue by the people is adopted as a measure. The entire canvas of problems related to coal mining emergency planning and disaster management have to be seen in the socio-politico economic background of this industry in India. An effective methodology of bottoms up information flow and top down planning processes based on an effective and efficient management information system and decision support system with provision of data capturing at source, is of prime importance. All these, however, will work only with a transformation in the working ethos in the coal mining industry that exists today.

The major disasters are taking place mostly in developing countries because it is not the disasters like earthquakes which kill the people but the weak buildings which collapse and kill the dwellers therein. Secondly though the prediction of the occurrence of earthquakes cannot be accurate, yet vulnerability assessment, warning and information system, inventory of all available resources at a particular place, drafting of action plan, rehearsal and drills by the local administration, etc., can certainly mitigate the effects of earthquakes of higher intensity.

The genesis and management of Anthropogenic and natural hazards in service/industry along with the growing dynamism in market economy industrial development and tourism in the last decade of the 20th century, have brought the role of service industry to a new zenith. Hotels and holiday resorts are one of the principal components in service industry and are hence spread over varied terrain and diverse cultural-cum-demographic agglomeration. The functioning of hotels/holiday resorts are hence in a state of dynamic equilibrium with essentially three disaster processes viz (i) man induced, (ii) human behavioural and (iii) natural through a host of hazards like waste generation, water shortage, fire, accidents due to failure of lift, accidents in swimming pool, harmful water quality of sea water on beaches, inadequate supportive infrastructural facility, induced slope failure scaling in pipes carrying water, algae generation, earthquake, etc. the disastrous approach of the tribal development has also been discussed vividly.

I would like to thank the entire typing and library staff of A.N. Sinha Institute of Social Sciences, without whose cooperation, my participation in the Congress would not be possible. The cooperation given by The A.N. Sinha Institute of Social Sciences and the UAES towards my endeavour has made my work a success.

Sachindra Narayan

List of Contributors

1. Dr. Sachindra Narayan, A.N. Sinha Institute of Social Studies, Patna-800001.
2. Mr. K.D. Sinha, I.A.S. Commissioner & Secretary Forest and Environment Department, 2M/6, Strand Road, Patna-800001.
3. Vinod K. Sharma—Anthropologist, Ranchi.
4. Shashi B. Sahai
5. Yuvaraj D. Prasad—Director A. N. Sinha, Institute of Social Studies, Patna-800001.
6. Prasanta Dutta—Prof. Patna University, Hurbur.
7. Dr. A.K. Jha, Head of Dept. of Political Science & Public Administration A.N.S. Institute of Social Studies, Patna-800001.
8. Mr. S.K. Choudhary, (C. Eng. (Lond) Former Chairman, Coal India Limited).
9. Dr. Govind P. Sharma, 1968, Lower Burdwan Compound, Ranchi-834001.
10. Mr. Subhas Sharma, 22/60 Officers Flats, Bailey Road, Patna, Bihar-800001.
11. Ms. Mamta Sinha, Hotel Maurya, Patna.
12. Dr. P.C. Oraon—Director Bihar Tribal Research Institute Ranchi.

1

Management of Disaster and Rehabilitation

SACHINDRA NARAYAN

Introduction

Anthropology the Science of Man in its totality has to deal with disaster management at the close of the millennium and have to equip for 21st century with management skills.

In tribal India, and also in other parts of the world, we frequently find drought, flood, epidemic, mysterious diseases leading to depopulation, migration and other allied problems.

The concept of tribe has drawn wide range of attention varying from anthropologists, administrators, policy makers, historians, members of judiciary, politicians, journalists, members of international bodies like UNESCO, Human Rights Commission, UNO, etc. But here we are using the term strictly in Anthropological terminology.

Generally speaking, by the term tribe we mean a group of people living at a particular place from time immemorial.

Anthropologically the tribe is a system of social organisation which includes several local groups, villages, bands, districts of lineages and normally includes a common territory, a common language and a common culture. The elements constituting the tribe may or may not be coordinated by formal or centralized political power, ideally the term 'tribe' implies large elements of solidarity based on strongly shared primary sentiments. Such solidarity becomes contractual in nature as the tribal organisation become more formally organised. The point at which these characteristics become pronounced is perhaps a convenient place to distinguish between the tribe and the nation. In general, anthropologists agree on the criteria by which a tribe may be described viz common territory, a tradition of common descent, common language, common culture, common name, political system, simple economy, religion and belief, primitive law and non-educational system.

Power is the ability to do something, strength, force, vigour, energy, ability to control or influence others, ability to impose one's will. Thereby, empowerment means inducing all these characteristics in an individual, social phenomenon, community, tribe, caste, racial ethnic group, etc., through planned systematic manner which may be termed as planning for the development of the people of a particular country, region, tribe, caste, etc. Thus, empowerment is an ability to control or influence or make the people willing for the development which may be economic, social, cultural or political.

Empowerment means putting the external force in an individual, tribe, caste, country, etc. to make him powerful. It is a process. It cannot be done in a day. It takes place systematically and scientifically. It is an experiment. If the chemical substances are mixed in proper order, then it is bound to be successful otherwise it will fail. Here comes the role of anthropologists and bureaucratic experts who have sufficient knowledge of social administration inputs like chemical substance. He knows in which or what cultural/social system how much typological variant chemical substances are required.

The various forms of power act and interact on each other so significantly, that if the study of power were confined to a single aspect, such as, political, economic or social power, much would be lost in the understanding of the overall dynamics of the system.

It is perhaps in social systems that the concept of power is most important. One of the great problems in constructing a general theory of power is the taxonomic difficulties. The very word power is used in variety of ways. In social system and human behaviour, there is a larger concept of power: to what extent and how we can get what we want? Within this there is smaller concept of power, somewhat beloved by anthropologist, which is our capacity to get other people to do things that contribute to what we want. There are three broad categories of power—threat power, economic power and integrative power. These are closely related to another tripartite division—the power to destroy, the power to produce and exchange and the power to integrate, that is, the power to create such relationships as love, respect, friendship, legitimacy and so on. Threat power is particularly the concern of political scientists, economic power of economists and the integrative power is the concern of anthropologists although it has not been studied very explicitly.

It is the integrative power that is the most dominant and significant form of power, in the sense that, neither threat power nor economic power can achieve very much in the absence of legitimacy, which is one of the more important aspects of integrative power. Without legitimacy, both threat and riches are 'naked'. The great fallacy specially of political thinking in regard to power, is to elevate threat power to the position of dominance which it does not really possess. Failure to understand this is an enormous source of error in human decisions, both at the individual level of those who control organisations, and at the group level which gets reflected in social control.

The work that comes closest to this argument is that of an important economist, John Kenneth Galbraith (1983). He too classifies power into three categories which he calls 'condigu', 'compensatory' and 'conditioned'. The terminology strikes me a little awkward but does correspond roughly to my threat, economic and integrative categories. Galbraith's book, as is to be expected, is full of useful insights, but does not develop the systematic structure that has been one of the principal concerns, particularly in regard to the dynamic aspects of the system.

Thus, it is clear that empowerment is the most elusive term. When additional input is provided to make a man powerful, it is known as empowering an individual, so is the case with a social phenomenon, social group, caste, tribe, man, woman, state, nation, etc. Empowerment means providing systematic developmental inputs to the target group. It is achieved through a continuous, systematic and scientific process. It is a part of the planning process for the development of mankind. While planning for the development of the target group, the desired development is expected through empowerment inputs.

Empowerment can be cultural, ethnic, educational, economic, political, health related, etc. It can be of many more types depending upon the requirement and suitability of the target group for whom the whole exercise of 'developmental planning' is done.

Now comes the question of empowering the tribals. Here we are using the term tribals strictly in anthropological terminology. For some, it may correspond to ethnic group or racial group but we will include them to the extent they fall within our term of reference.'

It is true that differential development has taken place at the global level among the tribes. Therefore, the necessity of this Commission has arisen in order to integrate them through the process of an empowerment which is the emerging need of 21st century of anthropology.

Disaster Management

The term disaster may be defined as an unexpected happening causing a huge loss of life and property. It may be both natural as well as man made in the sense that in some parts of the country, floods are coming due to the construction of check dams and embankments on the rivers. Disaster may come in the forms of earthquakes, cyclones, floods, drought, fire, etc. and ruin the life and property of the people. Anthropology is mainly concerned with through how to prevent, predict and mitigate major disasters? So far, scientific and technological development the prevention of earthquakes, cyclones, floods, droughts, fires, etc. may be prevented and predicted to some extent, but there is no doubt that proper planning and effective management can reduce the effects and hazards of disasters, since it is not the earthquake itself but the defective buildings which cause loss of life and property.

To prevent disaster, there should be pre-planning of all the available resources, communication facilities, manpower, etc. Experience has shown that before starting the rescue work administration has to clean the roads and bridges which are badly damaged. For this not only an inventory of local resource should be prepared but also bypasses and alternative routes should be identified in the plan itself. Since disaster is a state subject, the state government is responsible for rescue, relief and rehabilitation. However, at the national level ministry of agriculture, Government of India, is the nodal agency and there is one Crisis Management Committee in which all departments are represented along with Planning Commission. Recently the Finance Commission recommended for sharing of relief between the centre and state on 50:50 basis. Further there should be an emergency plan for each and every district in which response mechanism should be clearly spelt out. For instance what, how and when the relief is to be given, is to be specified. The allocation of work—who will do what; and clarification of organisation into: public, NGOs, army or civil administration should be properly undertaken otherwise the natural disaster results into chaos, anarchy and destruction due to confounded confusion. The price to pay for the demands imposed by mankind on our environment, extravagant to the point of profligacy, is increasing with time. It is the poorest who suffer the most, but all of us are caught up in the same syndrome. Humankind inherit but one earth, which they conspire against while destroying the gifts of nature by reducing the water-table, deforestation and pollution to name a few, which results in climatic changes and consequences measured in terms of human suffering which are likely to be acute.

The common view of disaster is due for a radical change. Though triggered of by natural events such as floods and earthquakes, disasters are increasingly man made. Some disasters (floods, droughts, famines) are caused more by environmental and resource mismanagement than by too much or too little rainfall. The impact of other disasters which are triggered by acts of nature (earthquake, volcano, hurricane) are magnified by unwise human actions. Disasters are social and political events which can be and often are prevented. In the Third World, where the poor are forced to overuse their land and live on dangerous grounds, disasters are taking a rising toll. By emphasizing mitigation instead of development, current disaster relief is often inadequate to the task it sets itself.

We can only tackle the root causes if disaster prevention and response are designed so as to incorporate both developmental and environmental strategies. We must get at the root causes and reverse the trends of increasing poverty and environmental degradation before it is too late. A sustainable eco-system must be our aim, as one in which the global family can live in balanced harmony with the whole of nature. The rural poor, who are the principal victims of the three elements which between them make up the major part of the Third World disasters—deforestations, soil erosion and desertification should be central to the work of all disaster agencies. All the trends emphasize that ignorance and grinding poverty accelerate the onslaught of disasters and exacerbate the cruel impact they have, particularly on vulnerable groups of people. The poor, the handicapped, the infant and the aged are the first to lose their basic right to food, shelter and health. They need and deserve our help. The social development of people and their communities in disaster prone areas has been grossly ignored by governments and agencies alike. Such appalling human conditions can best be fought through the weapons of self-reliance, literacy, preventive health care and equitable pricing structures for rural food producers, that is, helping people to respond to their own basic needs, within their environment.

The common view of natural disaster is due for a radical change. A new term may even be needed, such as 'nature disaster' to distinguish calamities associated with the forces of nature from such tribulations as war and factory explosions. Today humans are playing too large a role in natural disasters for us to go on calling them natural.

So a distinction must be made between the "trigger events" too little rain, too much rain, earthshocks, hurricanes—which may be natural and the associated disasters which may be largely man made. Scientists, politicians, decision makers and the general public have been very slow to make the basic distinction between the trigger and the disaster.

Most of the scientific effort and money devoted to natural disaster has been spent on studying climatological and geological triggers—over which humans have very little control—rather than on studying the wide range of human actions—over which humans do have some control—which bring more disasters upon people every year.

Contemporary natural disasters research has become the single greatest impediment to improvement in both the understanding of natural calamities and the strategies to alleviate them.

Researchers have concentrated on the physical aspects of disasters rather than the social and political aspects, governments have been lured into putting their trust in grand physical prevention and mitigation measures.

Despite the death, destruction and after affects of major natural disasters, they have received surprisingly little scientific attention. Science has not even had much success defining what it means by the term 'disaster'. Dictionaries use words such as 'misfortune' or 'calamity' implying, that for them to be a disaster, people must suffer. Thus, a cyclone or an earthquake is not a disaster unless it kills people or damages their property. This seems obvious but it is not since 1966 the UN Educational, Scientific and Cultural Organisation (UNESCO) has listed each year's natural disasters earthquakes, sunami (large ocean waves) storm surges and volcanic eruptions.

Other experts take almost the opposite view, defining disasters only in terms of their impact upon people. For instance, in order to produce some consistency in disasters, the Natural Hazard Research Group at the University of Colorado (US) came up in 1969 with the following definition of a disaster:

* more than $1 million in damage, or
* more than 100 people dead, or
* more than 100 people injured.

This definition had the effect of separating the disaster event—destruction, death and injuries from the trigger mechanisms— high winds, earth shocks, lack of rain, excess of water, lava and high waves. It also served to emphasize that most of research on disaster by climatologists and geologists is really on the trigger mechanisms. Other definition of disaster include:

"An event (or series of events) which seriously disrupts normal activities" Cisin and Clark (1962). "An accident on a new large scale" Walker (1973).

Tribals are unable to draw immediate attention of the policy makers, concerned government activists, anthropologists, etc. The ethnographic studies and the applied anthropology fail to cater to the needs of the tribals. Therefore, the anthropology of disaster management becomes a necessary dimension of Anthropology of 21st century: The century of Anthropology.

Anthropology of 21st century: The century of Anthropology has to widen its horizon according to need of the Man of 21st Century. The science celebrating its century has to be careful in selecting priorities of research and other academic pursuits.

The Indian anthropology will have to grow and shape its branches under the influence of world anthropology.

When one compares the number of people killed per disaster against the income of the country involved, one finds a steep rise in mortality with decreasing income. Gunnar Hagman of the Swedish Red Cross finds evidence that most disaster's are found in middle income countries and most property damage is caused in the rich nations. It is presumed that the middle income nations may have the most disaster events because of an aggressive economic development policy which includes over cultivation, deforestation and other forms of environmental degradation. Both Tokyo, Japan and Managua, Nicaragua are prone to earthquakes. But the people of Tokyo are far less vulnerable to injury by earthquake because Tokyo has strictly enforced building codes, zoning regulations and earthquake training and communications system. In Managua, there are still many people living in top heavy, mud brick houses on hillsides. They are vulnerable to such disasters.

The idea of anthropology of disaster management raises questions for the various groups interested in disasters.

* For governments: Can government be more effective in protecting its people from disasters by working to change patterns.
* For relief, aid and volunteer agencies active in disasters: Might it make more sense to invest some effort and funds in development before a disaster occurs, rather than putting all efforts after the event.
* For journalists: Is it enough to merely count the dead and describe the damage? or is it a journalists' job to look behind the scenes of destruction to expose ways in which people, politics and social systems have been responsible for any given disaster.
* For those responsible for development: Are they putting too much emphasis on "growth at any price", a policy which may have more and more people on the margins of society dangerously exposed to disasters?

Many people of the world, specially of Third World are more or less permanently affected by disaster processes and hundreds of millions are vulnerable to flood and droughts and to shortages of food, water and fuel wood. As natural disasters and many resource shortages are on the increase, it is obvious that the current development efforts are having little effect in these areas. This may be partly because rural development is rarely the priority it ought to be.

Prevention is urgent as the increasing frequency and severity of disasters are scaling the point of being unmanageable. In large parts of Asia, Africa and Latin America, the ecological base for human existence is being so damaged that it can no longer support the growing population of these regions.

Most disaster problems in the Third World are unsolved development problems. Disaster prevention and mitigation is thus primarily an aspect of development. Disasters can actually become "vehicles for change and involve both development and relief agencies in long-term programmes aimed both at development and at disaster prevention and mitigation.

Disasters are not unforeseen events and the technology now exists to identify the hazards that threaten a community and to estimate the areas and the settlements that will be affected. In most places and segments of society where calamities are occurring, the natural events are about as certain as anything within a person's lifetime. The very essence of disaster mitigation is long-term planning, while the very essence of Third World poverty is the struggle of day to day existence. The local people are more concerned with their children's education or lack of it, their health and the scarcity of medicine in the dispensaries and the difficulties of selling their crops at a decent price, which relates to the problems of access to markets in the accessible terrain. So vulnerability to natural hazards has to be recognised within the cultural and economic context of poverty and deprivation. And as with our own society, long-term logical action is frequently overwhelmed by short-term expediency.

Effective disaster mitigation and prevention depends on long-term planning for development towards a more sustainable and less vulnerable society. Some relief agencies are embarking on new types of community based disaster prevention programmes. Improved self-reliance in respect of food and fuel, access to land, employment, better health and nutrition, family planning and education are important components of disaster prevention. Disaster prevention and the elimination of poverty are closely linked as are poverty and environmental degradation. Many relief agencies are beginning to complement their emergency aid with their development programmes and are now working towards gaining knowledge, experience, training personnel and public backing to initiate new ideas into practice, in order to understand and minimize the problems of disasters.

Spread of AIDS : A Man Made Disaster

The anthropology of disaster management deals with both natural disaster as well as disaster created by Man. Prevalence of AIDS in Tribal India is an example of recent disaster created by Man.

Tragedy stares at India's tribal population in the face, as the virus that causes AIDS moves from red light areas and shady highway *dhabas* to tribal region. Yet amidst the suffering, people still find the strength to forgive, nurture and fight for their doomed families.

Specialists are grappling with the national implications of answers to combat the new threat that the Acquired Immune Deficiency Syndrome or AIDS cases pose in India. The attack of AIDS on tribals can clearly be visualized.

Officially the figures do not speak of Indian tribal population becoming AIDS newest victims as yet. The government funded National AIDS Control Organisation reports that at of the 2.9 million screened for the disease nationwide 49,327 tested positive for the human immuno deficiency virus (HIV). Of them 3,161 had progressed to AIDS in which the virus crippled their immune systems and exposes them to like tuberculosis and cancer.

Perhaps the most worrying aspect is the growing evidence in India of what HIV experts call "transmission chains" by which the virus percolates insidiously through social substrata and afflicts low risk individuals like housewives and children. In tribal area the HIV infected person very easily injects the disease of AIDS among women. The tribal women who are living close to urban or industrial centres, mines, etc., are quite often sexually exploited; and in some cases the exploiters are HIV positive persons.

Secondly large-scale migration of tribals from tribal region to Punjab, Haryana, Jammu and Kashmir, West Bengal, etc., are also contributing towards the sexual exploitation of the tribal women resulting in infection of AIDS.

Life of the Indian HIV victim ends the moments he tests positive. Illiteracy, social taboos and retrograde customs are just some of the barriers that confront those infected and those working to prevent the spread of the disease. At the beginning of the new millennium, India is projected to suffer one of the world's most rapid expansions of the HIV pandemic.

Rehabilitation and Displacement Perspective of Disaster

An anthropologist who is quite often turned into a social doctor looks at the problems of displacement and rehabilitation. Anthropological, psychological issues which are natural outcomes of displacement resulting in rehabilitation because of development projects are the subject matter of disaster management. It discusses anthropo-psychological consequences on the people affected by these projects and attempts to provide a basic framework to understand its anthropological perspective. It presents basic guidelines, action strategies for effective implementation of projects with a view to minimize advise anthropo-psychological effects on displaced population. It is also presumed that this will help those who are the key participants in planning and implementation of disaster projects.

Current Status of Displacement and Development

Development is an ongoing process which leads to commissioning of various kinds of development projects such as: Construction of new irrigation dams, establishing new factories, mines, road construction, railways and many other projects related to infrastructural growth leading to regional/ national economic development. This often necessitates the government to acquire land which leads to 'involuntary displacement' of people from the original home land.

Development leading to displacement of people from their own land is inevitable. All activities mentioned above, force the otherwise stable, sedentary population to move away from their original places of home and work. It uproots people from their original land and creates psycho-sociological stress leading to many dysfunctional consequences. More often, both social and economic benefits of such developmental projects are not shared equally by displaced population.

The problem of displacement is normally related to economic aspects but truly speaking, it has more of psycho-sociological implications. Though the meagre economic compensation provides temporary relief to evacuees, but it leads to many psycho-sociological and cultural problem of serious nature. The displacement demands change in the lifestyle of people and forces them to adjust in a totally alien social milieu. This causes a situation of psychological stress. Compulsory and involuntary displacement together with, 'rarely fair' payment of compensation are its two main reasons as a problem (Menezes, 1991). According to him, the current system fails to acknowledge that an 'oustee' is deprived of a historical right of access to a large number of resources, entire way of life and is not given any opportunity to demand an adequate price for this loss. Apart from his private land and cultural historical heritage, an oustee holds several other livelihood generating assets which are not legally acknowledged. Evidences suggest that these psycho-sociological problems are not well considered neither by the planners nor by those who are the key participants in the implementation of such projects. Therefore, the understanding and management of these problems are more important for effective implementation of these projects.

It is reported that accurate figures of displaced population are not available. Conservative estimate, reveal that around 15 million persons have been displaced from the first to sixth five-year plans. The real figure may be as high as 36 million. Despite the severity of the problems associated with displacement, the country lacks a reliable 'Data base' on the exact situation of displaced people (Vyas, 1993). The official sources, by and large, tend to underestimate the number of persons displaced by developmental projects. For example, different sources reveal different figures of the displaced people from construction of Hirakud Dam as shown in Table 1 (Government of Orissa Report, 1968; and Patnaik, Das and Mishra, 1987).

TABLE 1
DISPLACEMENT FIGURES OF HIRAKUD DAM PROJECT

Source	*Dam*	*No. of People Displaced*	*Land Submerged*
Govt. of Orissa Report (1968)	Hirakud Dam	1.1 lakh people	1,67,376,83 acres
Patnaik, Das and Mishra, (1987)	Hirakud Dam	1.1 lakh to 1.6 Lakh	1,82,592 acres

Displaced Population

The report of the Commissioner for Scheduled Castes and Scheduled Tribes (1990), points out that when the land is acquired and under the present law, only its property form is considered vital, questions concerning the very survival of the displaced persons are settled on this basis. Even those, who are identified, are very inadequately compensated. Lack of accurate data on such crucial issues, such as this, is itself an indication of both the Central and State governments degree of concern for the rehabilitation of oustees (Viegas, 1987). This current status of displacement is leading to an alarming situation. How to sustain the historical right which the oustee has been deprived of, is an important issue today.

Rehabilitation and Development

Rehabilitation is more often understood as economic rather than psycho-sociological phenomenon resulting from displacement. It is normally percèived as a 'planned change effort'. In a strict senses, it implies that, while there is a change the overall effects of the change is to restore the situation to its original condition. In other words, change or no change (Franks, 1991). Though rehabilitation is sought for development but its nature is quite different from other developmental processes. All developmental efforts imply planned change to improve existing conditions, whereas rehabilitation is designed to restore the status quo. This makes it imperative to understand the term rehabilitation in a much wider perspective, and its components which make it different from other developmental processes.

Components of Rehabilitation:

Rehabilitation can be described as having the following components[1]:

(i) Antecedent conditions: Displacement and rehabilitation of people are required when certain 'antecedent conditions' exist in the situation. For example, National long–term interest for socio-economic development of the country leading to commissioning of various developmental projects; National calamities, such as, war and political turmoil; Natural disasters, such as, floods, earthquakes, drought and also man made disasters.

1. The following format of conceptualization is partially adopted from the paper, Organizational Conflicts: Concepts and Models by Louis R. Pondy (1967).

(ii) Cognitive state of the individuals involved, i.e., their perception and awareness of the situation, such as:

* Fears and apprehensions about the possible problems to be faced by the affected people.
* Fears and apprehensions about their acceptability by the host population.
* Fears and apprehensions about fulfilment of government promises with respect to providing facilities.
* Attitudes about various 'developmental projects' and about 'government'.

(iii) Affective state of the individuals involved in the situation: Perception of a situation may affect the people in a variety of ways such as, developing anxieties, psychological tension, stress and hostility.

(iv) Manifest behaviour: Psychological effects manifest themselves in variety of behavioural patterns. These range from passive resistance to active resistance, overt aggression and finally agreeing for displacement under stress leading to many other dysfunctional behaviour patterns resulting in poor mental health.

(v) Rehabilitation: Displacement leading to rehabilitation of people through various rehabilitation programmes such as: Allotment of land: houses, monetary compensation, occupation and many other facilities required for resettlement.

(vi) Further demands by people from government: Any rehabilitation results in an aftermath which manifests itself in further demands by people from government.

Rehabilitation Process:

Drawing upon the ways in which components of rehabilitation are described, it is apparent that, displacement leading to rehabilitation can be described as a dynamic process having definite sequential stages coming one after the other. Each stage has its own characteristics which influences the process in its own way. Displacement leads to deterioration of the situation in the initial stages and subsequently to restoration of the situation, quite close to status quo. This is illustrated in Fig. 1.

Latent Stage
I

Cognitive Stage
II

Affective Stage
III

Manifest Stage, Leading to Displacement
IV

Rehabilitation Stage
V

Aftermath
VI

Fig. 1 Rehabilitation Process

Various stage depict:

I. Existing Stage, antecedent condition for displacement
II. Perception/Awareness of the situation
III. Affects on Individual
IV. Manifest Behavioural Patterns
V. Rehabilitation Programmes
VI. Further Problems/Demands.

Rehabilitation process comprises the following six stages:

(i) *Latent Stage:* It refers to the "Antecedent condition", for example, commissioning of developmental project leading to displacement and rehabilitation of population. The nature of antecedent condition will determine the ways of handling the situation in terms of "preparedness measures" and "coping strategies" by the government, other agencies, affected people and also by society. These will influence the characteristic pattern of behaviour of individuals at the next stage, which will also accordingly affect the "Preparedness measures and Coping strategies" for the subsequent stages leading to rehabilitation thereby characterized by certain stable aspects of condition, perceptions, affects and behaviour discussed later.

(ii) Cognitive Stage: Fears and apprehensions such as:

* Loss of home
* Loss of primary sources of gratification of needs
* Fear of change of basic style of living
* Loss or change in occupation (source of livelihood)
* Fear of adjustment in new jobs
* Loss of social relationships
* Fear of acceptability by the host population
* Lack of confidence in 'Government initiatives' and 'Programmes'.

All the above listed fears and apprehensions are the natural outcomes of displacement and are unavoidable. These must be acknowledged by all concerned. Correct diagnosis of the situation, appropriate 'preparedness measures' and 'coping strategies' to minimize them, can greatly reduce the severity of onset of next stage of the rehabilitation process.

(iii) Affective Stage: Perceived fears and threats may or may not affect the people equally under normal circumstances. These come on the surface and show up in various forms, such as, anxiety, tension, stress and may also lead to hostility. Effective handling of 'affective stage' would accordingly affect the state of next stage of the rehabilitation process.

(iv) Manifest Stage: Degree of psychological tension/stress will greatly influence the behavioural patterns at the manifest stage. People's passive and active resistance to 'evacuating the home land', and demand for better compensation may lead to aggressive behaviour and mass agitation. Quite often they finally agree for displacement under great stress leading to further deterioration of mental health.

(v) Rehabilitation Stage: This stage finally leads to rehabilitating displaced people through various 'Rehabilitation Programmes'.

(vi) Rehabilitation Aftermath: Howsoever effectively the various stages of rehabilitation process are handled, it

will still lead to an 'aftermath' in terms of further demands by the people leading to increased dependency on the government.

Psycho-sociological Consequences of Displacement

It is universally acknowledged that displacement is stressful and sometimes leads to traumatic conditions. In spite of this, the psycho-sociological issues have been neglected in the displacement of people under various projects. Rehabilitation programmes often lack specific components of the aspects of mental health of people. There is no evidence of discussion of the mental health problems and its implications for assessing cost and benefit of development projects.

A broadly defined psycho-sociological perspective can have important implications for designing rehabilitation policies. It allows us to anticipate inevitable problems that result from displacement of population to assess the consequence of particular policies.

A systematic analysis of what happens to individuals who are subjected to displacement from their homeland and require rehabilitation, will help us to provide the ways and means to minimize the adverse impact of involuntary displacement on mental health of people. Fears and apprehensions discussed earlier are usually perceived as potential threats by the affected population. These are natural and constitute the major components of displacement process resulting in dysfunctional behaviour patterns. These must be considered by all concerned involved in the management of the process. It is imperative to have indepth understanding of the consequences and subsequent careful handling, to minimize their adverse impact on mental health of people. This can be studied at two levels: Individual level and Group level.

Impact at Individual Level

Loss or Change in Primary Sources of Satisfaction of Needs:

The major fear associated with displacement is, loss or change in the primary sources of satisfaction of needs. All behaviours are instigated by needs and are directed towards goals that can satisfy these needs. Personality has a system of organized needs such as

(1) Physiological needs, e.g., thirst, hunger, sex etc.,

(2) Safety needs, e.g., security and order,

(3) Social needs, e.g., need to belong, identification and love,

(4) Esteem needs, e.g., need to achieve, need to control, self-respect and

(5) Self-actualisation, e.g., need for identity and self-fulfilment (Maslow, 1954).

Physiological needs are largely determined by the innate factors but others are greatly influenced by the nature of the social environment. Human beings are constantly seeking for pleasures, reflected through satisfaction of above mentioned needs in their unique manner through their established sources of livelihood, social relations, social status, kinship ties, etc. Any change or blockage, though temporarily, in the manner of satisfying these needs, will result in varying degrees of tension and stress in different people. Therefore, social environment together with the satisfaction of needs in an acceptable manner, become extremely important. For example, the satisfaction of the security need which constitutes an important need among the hierarchy of needs in Indian culture is greatly affected by the process of displacement. The compulsive change in the basic style of satisfaction of these needs is usually not welcomed by the people and hence often resisted. People may start perceiving themselves as having low self-worth, 'self-respect' and develop 'negative attitude' towards themselves. In an extreme situation, they may also develop identity crisis. All these result in lack of adjustment, leading to psychological stress or shock or trauma. The major factor associated with this is loss or change in the sources of occupation/livelihood leading to varying degrees of occupational redundancy and loss of social relationships.

(a) Change in Occupation/Livelihood

Fear of change of source of livelihood leads to

'Occupational disruption'. This may lead to low to high degree of 'Occupational redundancy'. This loss, even if substituted by the new ways of managing earning of livelihood, often leads to a state of mental stress. Loss of agricultural land by the landowners, though made up by 'Economic compensation' and also new occupational opportunities under various 'Rehabilitation programmes' by the government, could not fulfil the psychological loss such as, social status enjoyed through 'Feudalistic culture', and the village leadership leading to psychological satisfaction. All these sources of satisfaction of needs usually get blocked by the relocation process in the new environment.

Loss of land and property is a blow to the oustees, who are unable to secure an alternative source of livelihood because of lack of education and skill. Evidence suggests that many development projects created new occupational opportunities but the people were unable to get the share in the benefits of the project. The displaced persons, by and large, were forced into daily wage labour, for example, the persons displaced by the Pong Dam, who returned to Himachal Pradesh or decided to migrate to other states, in the hope of comparatively more comfortable life, were forced to become landless migrant labourers. Another example is that of 16,080 tribal families from 170 villages displaced by Ukai-Kakarpur Project on river Tapi in Gujarat. Surveys reported that 42 per cent of all the families, landed or landless were forced to migrate for work for varying periods of time, most of them in the sugar-cane factories (Mankodi and Gangopadhyay, 1983). All these occupational disruptions, especially loss of job/sources of livelihood, lead people to experience feelings of insecurity, defunctness, powerlessness and loss of self-confidence, leading to stress and in extreme cases, to psychological shock. The change in the job is also associated with variety of problems, such as, lack of skill and interest in the new job. Though people are provided training for the new jobs under various Occupational Rehabilitation Programmes, yet they are unable to use their potentials which demotivates them in the new jobs. They also develop feelings of low Self-efficacy (Grist,

1987)[2], Self-esteem (Brockner 1988)[3], Self-management (Manz & Sims, 1980)[4], Self-montoring (Snyder, 1987)[5], and Alienation, leading to a great stressful situation.

(b) Loss of Social Relationships

Displacement also forces individuals to change the pattern of social relationships, individuals have to undergo an entire process of resocialization and adjustment in a new social milieu. This leads to loss of existing social relationships. Kinship ties which are important sources of individual's gratification of social needs are in no way less important for an individual's survival. Evidence also suggests that the oustees are sometimes rejected by the parent group. The hostile behaviour of host population further makes the resocialization difficult for the oustees. Having faced rejection by the parent group and unacceptance by the host population, the oustees go through a tremendous psychological trauma and face an identity crisis. This sometimes leads people to go for second displacement, as in the case of Pong dam oustees (MARG, 1987).

Compensation Package:

Inadequate or in appropriate compensation package also results in psychological tension/stress among the oustees. It has been reported that adequate or inappropriate compensation packages to the oustees have also resulted in lot of psychological stress for the people. The illiterates found it difficult to utilize the compensation amount appropriately. This has led to social evils like alcoholism, gambling and prostitution (Advani, 1990).

Impact at Group Level

Displacement also results in disintegration of family, other social groups and occupational groups. Evidence from Augucha

2. Self-efficacy: Individual's belief that he is capable of performing a task in a new situation.
3. Self-esteem: Like or dislike themselves, expectations for success leads to risk taking.
4. Self-management: Ability to manipulate stimuli, internal process and responses to achieve personal behaviour outcomes.
5. Self-monitoring: Ability to adjust his behaviour to external situational factors (capacity for adaptation).

Mines of Hindustan Zinc Ltd., at Bhilwara, Rajasthan suggests that providing occupation to one representative of each evacuee's family by HZL, helped families, but created family tension resulting in breaking of joint family system and difficulties in getting match in their own community for their children (Advani, 1990).

All these psycho-sociological factors discussed above, result in psychological tensions, stress, hostility, sometimes leading to trauma. These get manifested in variety of dysfunctional behaviours leading to mental ill health and sometimès to mental sickness.[6]

Management of Displacement and Rehabilitation Process

In order to achieve the efficacy of various objectives of resettlement and rehabilitation projects, minimizing the adverse effects of displacement must form the primary focus. The success of these projects depends upon, how effectively the displacement is managed and the various rehabilitation programmes are perceived, as appropriate and adequate sources of gratification of needs by the affected population. This makes it imperative to plan, design and implement strategies as 'preparedness measures' and 'rehabilitation programmes', to cope with negative aspects of displacement, at the appropriate stages of the rehabilitation process.

Need for a 'National Policy'

Recognizing the adverse impact on human beings, the sufferings and hardships caused by involuntary settlement,

6. Mental health refers to certain sets of criteria. These are attitudes towards self, which include accessibility of the self to consciousness, correctness of the self-concept, self-acceptance and a sense of identity growth development and self-actualisation, which includes—concept of self, motivational processes and investment in living; Integration, which refers to balance of psychic-forces in the individual, unifying outlook to life and resistance to stress; Autonomy, which refers to decision-making process, regulation from within; Undistorted perception of reality including—empathy and social sensitivity; Environmental Master including ability to love, adequacy in inter-personal relations and efficiency in meeting situations requirement, capacity for adaptation and adjustment, efficiency in problem solving, adequacy in love, work and play.

the World Bank Policy states as its first requirement, that "whenever feasible, the involuntary resettlement must be avoided or minimized and alternative developmental solutions must be explored" (Cemea, 1988). Notwithstanding this policy, there have been cases, when projects have been designed and approved without examining such possible alternatives. Lack of provision of psycho-sociological consideration in the Land Acquisition Law 1994 and also 'Land Acquisition Amendment Act 1984, further weakens the implementation of the Bank Policy. Though rehabilitation has normally been envisaged as a planned change effort, evidences suggest that implementation of each project, called for an ad hoc policy of its own. The Bank Policy can be made effective only, if a well-defined National Policy is designed. Introducing of psycho-sociological perspective in the Land Acquisition Law will also greatly enhance the efficacy of bank policy. Therefore, the need for a well-defined national policy is a first pre-requisite for effective implementation of resettlement and rehabilitation projects.

Strategies for Minimizing Psycho-Sociological Consequences of Resettlement at Various Stages of Rehabilitation Process.

(a) Latent Stage

Nature of 'Antecedent condition' determines the ways and means of managing resettlement and rehabilitation process. Preparedness measures and coping strategies, need to focus around the factors leading to displacement and their counter impact on population. The rehabilitation process must be pursued with a developmental objective rather than merely as coping mechanism in the situation. All preparedness measures and coping strategies at each stage of the process, must reflect the achievement of the developmental objective. These must provide if not better, but almost similar physical amenities and sources of livelihood, by restoring quite close to the status quo and then focusing on further development of the people. Therefore, appropriate interventions at Government level, NGOs level, affected population level and other community level, become very important and can make displacement little easier for the people. Table 2 shows the management of various stages of rehabilitation process.

(b) Cognitive and Affective Stage

Disastrous psychological effects on people start showing up in the population to be displaced in the form of tension and stress even before the actual onset of displacement. Issue of the evacuation notices to the people for acquiring the land is the beginning of the psychological problems of the people. The degree of stress and tension which the people experience at this stage, because of inherent fears and threats, should be the focus of designing management strategies. Therefore, reduction of this state of tension and stress become extremely important.

Appropriate preparedness measures needed to be designed at this stage are under:

Preparedness Measures

Preparedness measures must focus around issues like:

(i) Prepare individuals psychologically to agree for displacement without much resistance.

(ii) Dissemination of timely information about displacement.

(iii) Minimising adverse impact on people.

Conscious efforts at all levels are required to formulate motivational strategies, around perceived potential fears and threats by the people. The following 'Operational Interventions' are needed at this stage:

Operational Interventions

Detailed Microlevel Planning

Detailed Planning in advance, before the onset of

TABLE 2

MANAGEMENT OF REHABILITATION PROCESS

Well Defined National Policy	*Latent Stage I*	*Antecedent Condition*
		*Acquisition of Land Leading to Displacement
PREPAREDNESS MEASURES OBJECTIVE	COGNITIVE STAGE II	PERCEPTIONS/ AWARENESS OF SITUATION

(Continued on next page)

TABLE 2 *Contd.*

*Preparing individuals of displacement		
*Dissemination of timely information about displacement		*Fears and Apprehension About
*Minimizing adverse impact on people		*Possible Problem
		*Fulfilment of Government promises
OPERATIONAL INTERVENTION		*Acceptability of host population
*Detailed micro level planning		*Attitudes about development projects
*Communication Strategy		
*People's Participation		
ROLE OF GOVT./NGO'S/OTHER AGENCIES COMMUNITY AND HOST POPULATION	AFFECTIVE STAGE III	DEVELOPING
		*Anxiety
		*Physiological Tension
		*Stress
		*Hostility
		*Shock/Trauma
MANAGEMENT STRATEGY	MANIFEST STAGE IV DISPLACEMENT	BEHAVIOURAL PATTERNS
*Negotiations with government. Affected people local leaders, other influential people of the area and NGO's		*Passive Resistance
	REHA- BILITATION	*Active Resistance
	STAGE–V	*Overt Aggression leading to mass agitation
*Taking help from: Social research organizations and other agencies for conducting social survey.		*Agreeing of displacement under stress
*Rehabilitating displaced	REHA- BILITATION STAGE VI	

displacement, should necessarily form an integral part of the process. The government must procure the data regarding the following aspects about the population to be displaced.

(i) Correct estimate of land to be acquired.

(ii) Number of households/families to be displaced.

(iii) Housing pattern of the area.

(iv) Population structure of the place: adults, males, females, children and old people.

(v) Caste structure of the area.

(vi) Educational profile of the people.

(vii) Professional skills available with the people.

(viii) Aptitudes and potentials available with the people.

(ix) Correct estimate of movable and immovable property with the people.

(x) Schools, hospitals, temples, transport and other facilities available to the people in the area.

(xi) Attitude of the host population to know acceptability of the displaced population.

The services of research organizations and other agencies can be of immense help in this regard.

All this data will provide the guidelines to decide the nature of compensation package and facilities to be offered to the people. It will also enable the government to design appropriate communication strategy to create a desirable impact over the people in generating positive outlook about displacement.

Communication Strategy: Communication strategy should have the following objectives:

(a) Developing awareness among individuals about need for displacement.

(b) Providing knowledge about the rehabilitation package and its commitment benefits to people.

(c) Preparing individuals psychologically to cope with the unwanted psychological stress.

(d) Preparing host population for accepting the displaced people.

People's Participation: People's participation should be the core managing technique in designing as well as implementation of communication strategy. All castes, different occupational groups, local leaders and other influential people who are key participants in day-to-day functioning of the affected area, should be represented in the rehabilitation process. Resettlement and rehabilitation plans about site for resettlement of people, housing pattern, compensation packages and other facilities should be drawn in consultation with the core participative group. People's involvement would enable the government to elicit commitment and would make the displacement less uncomfortable for people.

Procuring all this data from the people before the onset of displacement can provide a glimpse of government's sincere intentions and efforts of rehabilitating the people after displacement. This will have a positive impact on people and would considerably reduce the adverse affects of displacement.

(c) Manifest Stage

Careful and timely handling of cognitive and affective stage through appropriate preparedness measures would greatly reduce the psychological tension and stress generating dysfunctional behaviour at the manifest stage. In many cases the government has taken an unduly long time in deciding the compensation package, forcibly evacuated the people and acquired the land. Evidences suggest that people have shown their actual resistance and resorted to mass agitation under certain development projects. Such a situation can be effectively handled through negotiations between government and affected population. All infrastructural facilities such as land, houses, schools, hospitals, etc., should be provided to people before displacement. This would help in minimizing resistance.

(d) Rehabilitation Stage

Rehabilitation programmes necessarily need to be designed according to the felt needs of the affected population. Data about population, procured earlier as preparedness measures, must be appropriately used for designing the programmes.

Rehabilitation programmes should make use of available skills and talents and also focus upon providing new skills and competencies to the affected population, to equip them to face the outer world. Efforts should be made to develop settler's commitment to self-support and sustenance, to avoid onset of settlers dependency syndrome psycho-therapeutic/health programmes in the form of family counselling, stress reducing exercises, community programmes and other socio-occupational programmes should form an essential complement of the rehabilitation package along with adequate compensation package. The perception of compensation package, as adequate and good, is greatly influenced by, how effectively the psychological tension, stress and traumatic situation is handled through these programmes.

(e) Rehabilitation Aftermath

Effective management of earlier stages will greatly reduce the further demands by the people from the government.

Conclusion

The population which is more often displaced by the developmental projects usually belong to lower strata of society, such as Scheduled Castes and Scheduled Tribes who are more affected as compared to other displaced population. Therefore, as a part of socio-economic development, it must concern with safeguarding the interests of minority, the affected population, and minimizing the negative impacts of relocations.

In spite of intentions of the government to provide a comfortable rehabilitation to the affected population, no attention has been paid to the psycho-sociological consequences associated with the process. Though rehabilitation projects are often viewed as a planned change effort with developmental objectives, they are rarely implemented in a manner to achieve those objectives. People have been made to evacuate from their land forcefully and have been made to experience psychological shocks, undergo trauma, more often resulting in mental illness. In fact, if these psychological consequences are not effectively handled, perhaps, new resettlement colonies created under the so-called development projects, having objectives of overall development of people, for better quality of life, leading to national development, will turn into mental asylums. It is, therefore, the right time to reflect on this problem and seriously evaluate the extent to which the policies, planning and strategies together, with their implementation by the government, have been inadequate and draw lessons for further action.

All managers, who are responsible for managing rehabilitation of people and concerned community, must appreciate and understand the complex psycho-sociological nature of displacement. Rehabilitation must be addressed as a planned changed effort, having sequential stages requiring detailed advance planning for each stage. Steps are needed to arrest the psychological consequences resulting at each stage. This requires correct diagnosis, designing and implementing appropriate interventions as preparedness measures and coping strategies.

It is believed that the perspective presented and guidelines suggested in this chapter are functional and would be able to solve many of the deficiencies of the current management approach to problems associated with displacement and rehabilitation.

REFERENCES

Advani, Mohan: Socio-economic Aspects of Resettlement and Rehabilitation: A Study of Rampura Augucha Mines, Udaipur, Samaj-Shastra Hindi Karya Samiti, 1990.

Brockner, J.: *Self Esteem at Work*, Lexington: MA, Lexington Books, Chapts. 1-4, 1988.

Cemea, Michael, M.: *Involuntary Resettlement in Development Projects*, World Bank Technical Paper Number 80, Washington: World Bank, 4, 1988.

Cisin and Clark, 1962, *Man and Society in Disaster*.

Commissioner for Scheduled Castes and Scheduled Tribes. Twenty-ninth report of the Commissioner for SC and ST, New Delhi: The Manager of Publications, Government of India, 245, 1987-89.

Franks, Tom: *Institutional Change and Project Rehabilitation, Hardware, Software and Liveware, in Project Rehabilitation in Development Countries*, ed. by Colin, Kirkpatrick, London: Routledge 213, 1991.

Galbraith, John Kenneth, 1983. *The Anatoney of Power*, Boston: Houghton Hifflin.

Gist, M.E.: Self Efficacy: Implementation for Organization Behaviour and Human Resource Management, *Academy of Management Review*, July, 472-85, 1987.

Government of Orissa: Report on the Benefits of Hirakud Irrigation: A Socio-economic Study, Cuttack: Bureau of Statistics and Economics, Government of Orissa, 13, 1968.

Jahoda, Marie: Current Concepts of Positive Mental Health, Joint Commission on Mental Illness and Health, Monograph Series, No. 1, New York: Basic Books, 1958.

Mankodi, Kashyap and Tanushree, Gangopadhyay: *Rehabilitation: The Ecology and Economic Costs*, Surat: Centre for Social Studies, 81, 1982.

Manz, C.C. and H.P. Sims: "Self management as a substitute for leadership: A social learning theory perspective." *Academy of Management* Review, July, 361-67, 1980.

MARG: *Pong Dam* Oustees, New Delhi, Multiple Action Research Group Mimeo, 1987.

MARG: *The Land Acquisition Act and you*, New Delhi: Pauls Press, 1990.

Maslow, K.H.: *Motivation and Personality*, New York, Harper and Bros., 1951.

Menezes, Arul: Compensation for project displacement: A new approach, *Economic and Political Weekly*, 26 (3): 2465-2469, 1991.

Narayan, Sachindra: *Indian Anthropology,* Gyan Publishing House, New Delhi.

——————: *Dimensions of Development of Tribal Bihar*, Inter India Publications, New Delhi.

——————: *A Dwindling Tribe of Bihar*, Naya Prakash Sauria Paharia, Calcutta.

Patnaik, S.K., B. Das, and A. Mishra: 'Hirakud Dam Project: Expectation and Realities' In PRIA (ed) *People and Dams*, New Delhi: Society for Participation Research in Asia: 47-59, 1987.

Pondy Louis, R: "Organization Conflict: Concept and Models." *Administrative Science Quarterly*, 12 (2), 296-320, 1967.

Snyder, M.: *Public Appearances / Private Realities: The Psychology of Self-Monitoring*. New York: W. H. Freeman, 1987.

Viegas, Philip: The Hirakud Dam Oustees: Thirty Years After, New Delhi: Multiple Action Research Group (mimeo), 1987.

Vyas, H. N.: Displacement, Compensation and Rehabilitation: A Study of Submergence Area Evacuees, Ph.D. Thesis in Sociology, Udaipur, Mohanlal Sukhadia University (Unpublished), 1993.

2

Ethnicity–Policy Gap Problem Management

K.D. SINHA, I.A.S.

The Chotanagpur plateau of Bihar is predominantly inhabited by tribals. This area is very rich in minerals and has huge area of forest. Only 30 per cent of the land is under regular cultivation. There is ample scope for development of land in this area.

This area has got vast deposit of coal, iron ore, copper and other minerals. In the last 50 years, a large number of mines have been opened in this area and in future also this area will witness mining activities on a large scale.

People of this area are generally engaged in the cultivation of land. They have got customary rights in certain forest produce and enjoy some concessions for using products from the forest area. They have got legal rights to develop the land in and around their villages for the purpose of cultivation. Their main occupation is farming and they meet their subsistence needs by growing crops through family labour. They grow fruit trees in the compound of their houses. They are very good cultivators. They also use forest produce for supplementing their domestic requirements. They rear cattle which produce milk and organic manure. The cattle depend on trees, shrubs, bushes and grass for their fodder. Fuel- wood is grown in the forest and the land near their habitation. They have got right to collect firewood from the forest for their personal use. Thus, the natural resources provide them not only a means of subsistence but also offer opportunities to increase their income by reclamation and development of land which is available in plenty.

On the basis of the natural resources available in the area, a social hierarchy has developed among different groups of people. The economic activity is the basic determinant of this hierarchy. Social status is based on the ownership of land, their capacity to grow crops and the resources that they have for this purpose. The highest ambition of the people of this area is to possess land, be a producer and live a self-supporting life.

Literacy among these people is very low. Villages are smalls having a population of about 300-400 persons. Education and vocational skill among these people is negligible. Their main expertise lies in managing agricultural land, growing subsistence crops and undertaking horticulture activities.

Due to rich deposit of minerals in this area open-cast mines have been and are being started in large numbers which necessitates acquisition of land on a large-scale. Every year, huge area of agricultural, forest and other land is being acquired, with the consequence, a number of people have lost their livelihood. In many cases, the entire village along with the cultivable land is acquired giving rise to the problem of displacement and rehabilitation. Mining activities also lead to the destruction of forest on which, as mentioned earlier, the local people depend for meeting their various day to day requirements.

Among mining operations undertaken in this area the most important one is related to extraction of coal. Most of the coal mines are opencast mines. For this purpose land has been acquired on a large-scale. Opencast mines are worked by breaking the surface of the land and thereafter, overburden is removed. Approach roads to the mines are constructed generally by using locally available materials like moram, sand, earth, etc. For working the mines and extracting the coal, big machines are employed. In many cases manual labour is also used for this purpose. Coal is generally carried manually by the labourers in baskets.

On account of the large-scale acquisition of land, the local residents lose their cultivable land. Many times the residential area is also acquired. Thus, the opening of coal mines results in loss of livelihood and creates problems of resettling them at new places. Coal mining also leads to environmental degradation. The trees are cut in large numbers and overburden is dumped at various places. The air is full of dust. The operation of big machines, trucks, dumpers and bulldozers used for mining and carrying coal create noise pollution. The underground water table goes down due to digging of big pits leading to scarcity of water in the area. The area becomes inhabitable and people suffer from various physical ailments.

In order to solve the problem arising out of the opening of coal mines, various schemes of rehabilitation have been taken up in the past. Generally the demand of the local people is that they should be given cultivable land in adjoining areas. However, this demand cannot be met due to non-availability of cultivable land in adequate measure. The other option is that they should be given the jobs created by the operation of the coal mines. In the first instance, since the coal mines are gradually being mechanized, the number of unskilled jobs is declining. So far as skilled jobs are concerned, people are recruited from the national labour market, where the local people have very little chance of competing. Some skilled jobs require training in various trades. The people inhabiting these areas are generally illiterate and do not have any training for doing skilled or semi-skilled work. The jobs are also of various types. There is no institution which can provide training to the local residents for large number of trades and vocations at one place. Thus, the local people get employment only as unskilled labourers which generally consists of carrying coal and overburden materials on head and other works which can be done manually. Even these works are unavailable in plenty. In many cases when new mines are opened, the labourers are brought from old collieries having surplus manpower. Many works are given to private contractors. Such works are seasonal in nature and provide short-term employment. It has been found that all the jobs whether as skilled, semi-skilled, unskilled, casual, and seasonal, taken together are unsufficient to provide employment to the persons affected by acquisition of land.

Another feature of the rehabilitation scheme is that job is given to one person of the family if a minimum land of three acres is acquired. Since landholding of the family in these areas is small, it is impossible to give jobs to all the adults in the family. In most of the cases, employment is offered to one person which creates immense friction and ill will in the family. As agriculturists, income and agricultural produce is jointly owned by all members of the family and their consumption and other needs are met in an equitable manner. All the members work on the land for growing crops and participation in the management of agriculture operations. However, under the rehabilitation scheme offering employment only to one or two persons in the family, there is a tendency on their part to corner all the benefits of employment for themselves with the result that other persons face acute hardships. In some cases the employed member initially looks after the entire family and shares the income with other members but this arrangement does not continue for a long time as the income accruing may not be sufficient for all the members of the family and gradually a feeling develops in him that he is making immense sacrifice for other members of the family. Thus, the present scheme of offering employment to persons on the basis if minimum land to be acquired, creates friction and tension in the family life and eventually leads to break-up of the family.

Apart from mining activities, employment is generated due to construction of buildings for offices, residential houses for officers, employees and labourers. In order to cater to the day to day needs of various categories of the people viz workers, transporters and other persons engaged for the mining operation, small shops also come up. Many persons working in the coal mines require help from domestic servants for their household work. Thus, employment opportunities are created by these activities but these are also not adequate for the large number of persons affected by land acquisition.

If the nature of these jobs is analysed, it is found that most of these offer employment for a short period. These jobs are basically manual in nature and do not enjoy any respectability in the society. These jobs do not lead to upward social mobility. Given the opportunity the people will not like to take up the jobs of manual workers, domestic servants, sweepers, cleaners, etc. It has also been found that most of these people do not have the acumen to run shops and undertake business activities. However, in absence of better opportunities, they do accept these jobs grudgingly in order to make a living.

The justification given for setting up coal mining projects is that these will lead to overall development of the area. The people will benefit from the supply of electricity. There will be better educational and health facilities. Lot of employment opportunities will be created. These projects are essential for higher coal production which is needed for the development of the country. Through trickle down effect the area where the coal mines are located will also get substantial benefits and the local people will have a higher standard of living. It will open the door of prosperity and will augment their income. They are told to bear the hardships caused due to land acquisition and the resulting loss of livelihood in the initial stage with the hope that the project will ultimately bring economic benefits, create facilities for education, health, transport and housing and conditions for better living. What happens ultimately is that the promised development benefits do not reach them and they also lose the land, which is their permanent source of income. Electricity does not come to their villages even though the colliery area is electrified. Some schools are set up by the project authorities for the employees of the project but not for the local people. The children of local villages do not get admission in these schools. Similarly they are not entitled to get treatment in the hospitals set up by the project authorities which are, as mentioned earlier, meant for the employees and regular workers of the projects. The responsibility of the development of the area lies with State Government, not with the project authorities. Therefore, no development activities are undertaken by the project authorities and their concern is mainly limited to the production of coal. So far as the State Government is concerned, it has got its own priorities and more often than not, the village affected by these projects may not constitute the priorities for the government, as these villages have to be considered along with other villages of the State and decisions are taken on the basis of norms for ensuring objectivity, fairness and transparency in the selection of schemes for education, health roads, electrification and other sectors. Other villages of the state compete with these villages on equal terms. The trickle down effect depends on the rate of growth of the economy of the country as a whole and it may take several years for the benefits of the development to reach the local population in a significant manner. Thus, development remains a promise whereas the people suffer in various ways.

In all such projects, there are two main agencies, one the Project authorities and the other the State Government. The perceptions of both these agencies are different. The coal companies are primarily interested in coal production and the welfare and development of the local people are not regarded by them to be falling within their sphere of activity. They expect that their problems will be tackled by the State Government which should invest the necessary funds and create the infrastructure for this purpose. The State Government has been generally taking the stand that the fund for rehabilitation should come from the project and be treated as a part of project cost and that in view of the fact that the project authorities are the main beneficiaries of the production of coal, in terms of income, they should develop the project area. Building of infrastructure facilities for education, health, roads, etc., is highly capital intensive and with the resources at their command and the number of villages to be covered, the State Governments may not be able to discharge this onerous responsibility. The State Governments also believe that these projects will create, substantial employment opportunities for the people of the project area which they will be able to take advantage of. However, in practice, it does not happen. Training is also required for the local people for development of skills in order to make them suitable for employment available in the project. A large investment is generally required for undertaking such activities and the State Governments are not in a position to shoulder such a huge financial liability. Thus, whereas the coal companies are interested in the production of coal, the State Governments are more concerned with the rehabilitation of the displaced persons, creation of jobs, employment of the local people and creation of infrastructure facilities and overall development of the project area.

In this way, the opening of the project leads to unwholesome change in the living pattern, loss of social status, bleak future fraught with uncertainties, environmental degradation and break-up of family life and social fabric. As time passes, the above facts become more obvious to the local people. It generates tension and hostility among them towards the projects authorities. Their wrath, anger and despair find expression in violent acts directed against the people working in the project. This has led to physical assaults of the project authorities. The local people often obstruct roads and create conditions to hamper the running of the project. A feeling of insecurity prevails among the people working in the project. Both the local people and the project authorities find themselves completely at a loss at the adverse impact created by the project and do not know how to find a solution to the problem facing them.

The foregoing discussions lead to a theoretical model of sharing of revenue generated by the project with the various groups. The model also takes into consideration the anthropological perspective and provides solution to problems of development management which are essential for human welfare and desired change.

Various solutions, as discussed earlier, have been attempted like giving employment to limited number of people, compensation and rehabilitation at places where land is available. It is accepted by all that the project cannot offer employment to all the people affected. The jobs available do not lead to upward social mobility and economic prosperity. The places of rehabilitation are more often than not far away from their habitations and require lot of investment for making them inhabitable. The rehabilitation schemes require huge amount of money for their execution. The development remains a mere promise to the local people. The only way in which the project can be made meaningful to them is that the revenue generated by the project is shared with the local people. A part of the revenue earned by the project should be used for developing the village and providing means of livelihood to the affected people. There should be one authority or agency which should look after the rehabilitation, creation of jobs, employment, education and all the problems of the displaced persons. It should administer the project and develop the area in such a manner that the local people may become direct beneficiaries of the revenue generated by the project. The concept of revenue sharing will create stakes of the local people in the project and will also permit them to adopt a development pattern suitable for meeting their present and future needs and realizing their social and economic aspirations. This authority should participate in the management and have a substantive say in the running of the project. There should be adequate representation of the local people in authority or the agency. The revenue earmarked for the local people should be channelized through the authority.

3

Natural Disaster Management in India

VINOD K. SHARMA

Introduction

The unique geoclimatic conditions of the Indian sub-continent make this region among the most vulnerable to natural disasters in the world. Disasters occur with amazing frequency and while the community at large has adapted itself to these regular occurrences, the economic and social costs continue to mount year after year.

The Indian subcontinent is highly vulnerable to drought, floods, cyclones and earthquakes, though landslides, avalanches and bush fires frequently occur in the Himalayan region of northern India. Of the 31 States/Union territories in the country, 22 are disaster-prone.

Floods and Earthquakes

Among all the disasters that occur in the country, river floods are the most frequent and often the most devastating. The cause for floods is chiefly the peculiarities of rainfall in the country. Out of the total annual rainfall in the country, 75 per cent is concentrated over a short monsoon season of three to four months. As a result, there is a very heavy discharge from the rivers during this period causing widespread floods. As much as 40 million hectares of land in the country has been identified as flood-prone. An average of 18.6 million hectares of land is flooded annually. Floods are caused mainly in the Ganga-Brahmaputra-Meghna basin which carry 60 per cent of the nation's total river flow.

Earthquakes are considered to be one of the most dangerous and destructive natural hazards. The impact of this phenomena is sudden with little or no warning, making it just impossible to predict or make preparations against damages and collapses of buildings and other man-made structures. About 50-60 per cent of total area of the country is vulnerable to seismic activity of varying intensities. Most of the vulnerable areas are generally located in Himalayan and sub-Himalayan regions, and in Andaman and Nicobar Islands.

Droughts and Cyclones

Drought is a perennial feature in some states of India. Sixteen per cent of the country's total area is drought-prone and approximately 50 million people are annually affected by droughts. In fact, drought is a significant environmental problem too as it is caused by a less than average rainfall over a long period of time. In India, about 68 per cent of total sown area of the country is drought-prone. Most of the drought-prone areas identified by Government of India lie in the arid, semi-arid and sub-humid areas of the country.

India has a very long coastline of 5700 kms which is exposed to tropical cyclones arising in the Bay of Bengal and Arabian Sea. The Indian Ocean is one of the six major cyclone-prone regions of the world. In India, cyclones occur usually between April and May, and also between October and December. The eastern coastline is more prone to cyclones as about 80 per cent of total cyclones generated in the region hit there.

Natural Disaster Management at International Level

The United Nations Initiative

Natural Disasters are a global phenomenon and strike regardless of any national boundaries or socio-economic status of the region. This has led to a strong international fraternity defined at the highest level by several UN bodies. Interestingly, the United Nations declared the decade from 1990 till 2000 as the International Decade for Natural Disaster Reduction

(IDNDR). The objective of the IDNDR is to reduce through concerted international action, especially in the developing countries, the loss of life, property damage and social and economic disruption caused by natural disasters.

As per the plan of the IDNDR, by the year 2000 all countries should have (1) comprehensive national assessments of risks from natural hazards, with these assessments taken into account on development plans; (2) mitigation plans at national and/or local levels, involving long-term prevention and preparedness and community awareness; and (3) ready access to global, regional, national and local warning systems and broad dissemination of warnings.

The last major conference of the IDNDR programme was held in Yokohama in May 1994, where a plan of action for disaster reduction, called the 'Yokohama Strategy' was evolved. The Yokohama strategy gave guidelines for natural disaster prevention, preparedness and mitigation. India was an active participant in the said conference and in the formulation of the guidelines. By doing so, it has recognized the need for further improvements in its disaster management mechanism and to develop a strong political will by way of a sound national policy in this regard.

Natural Disaster Management in India

India is a parliamentary democracy with a federal structure. An integrated disaster management mechanism exists within government framework. The essential responsibility of disaster management lies with the State Government where the disaster has occurred. However, in the event of disasters which spread over several states and assume uncontrolable proportions, the Central Government may be required to supplement appropriate measures in the fields of rescue, relief and preparedness. At the Central level, the National Crisis Management Committee (NCMC) oversees all disaster related efforts. The NCMC comprises the nodal ministry and other support ministries. For natural disasters, the nodal ministry is ministry of agriculture.

In the past, the government response to natural disasters has improved in terms of its effectiveness. This is chiefly due to the emergence of well-organized administrative machinery, presence of Relief Manuals at district level, predetermined allocation of duties and recognized public-private partnerships. However, absence of an integrated policy at national level has led to overlooking of some of the vital aspects of disaster management. As such, presence of a policy helps clearly define the government's basic approaches on a continuing basis. It provides for an appropriate legislation and associated regulations in this regard, besides providing an overall national competence and self-reliance vis-a-vis international initiatives.

Administrative Structure at Central Level

In the federal set-up of India, the responsibility to formulate the Government's response to a natural calamity is essentially that of the concerned State Government. However, the Central Government, with its resources, physical and financial, does provide the needed help and assistance to buttress relief efforts in the wake of major natural disasters. The dimensions of the response at the level of Central Government are determined in accordance with the existing policy of financing the relief expenditure and keeping in view the factors, like: (1) the gravity of a natural calamity; (2) the scale of the relief operation necessary, (3) the requirements of Central assistance for augmenting the financial resources at the disposal of the State Government.

Agriculture Ministry—The Nodal Agency

The Department of Agriculture and Co-operation (DAC), in the Agriculture Ministry, is the nodal department for all matters concerning natural disasters relief at the Centre. The National Contingency Action Plan (CAP) facilitates launching of relief and rescue operations without delay. The CAP identifies initiatives required to be taken by various Central Ministries, and Public departments in the wake of natural calamities, sets down procedures and determines the focal points in the administrative machinery.

In the DAC, the Relief Commissioner functions as the nodal officer to coordinate relief operations for all natural disasters. The Central Relief Commissioner receives information relating to forecast of the natural calamity from the Director General, Indian Meteorological Department from the Central Water Commission on a continuing basis. Agriculture Department monitors the developments taking place and provides the necessary inputs through the Agriculture Secretary to the Agriculture Minister, Prime Minister and the Cabinet.

The entire network of natural disaster management at Central level and the interaction pattern among various functionaries during the emergency period is shown below:

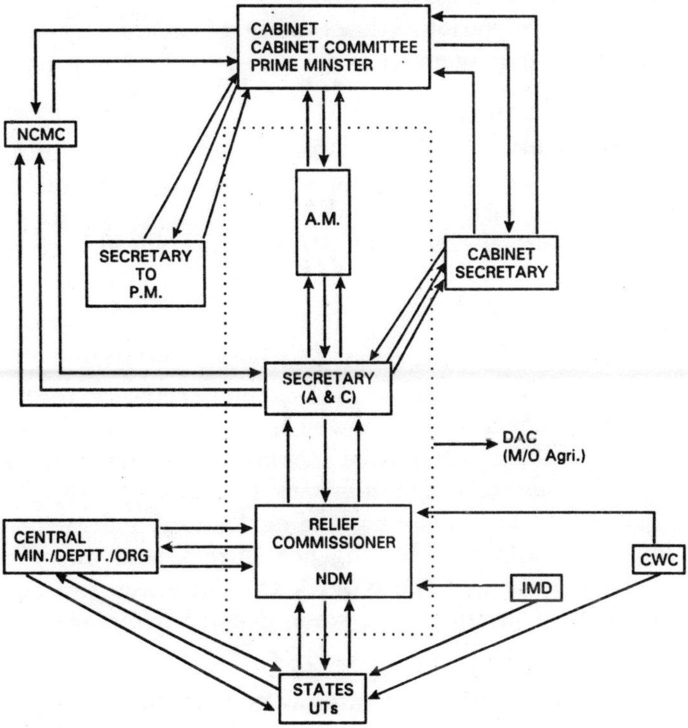

LEGEND ____________________

INFORMATION FLOW ____________________

INSTRUCTION/DIRECTION ____________________

FEED BACK ____________________

IMD	: Indian Meteorological Department
CWC	: Central Water Commission
NCMC	: National Crisis Management Committee
A.M.	: Agriculture Minister
P.M.	: Prime Minister
A. & C.	: Agriculture and Cooperation
N.D.M.	: Natural Disaster Management

Fig. 1. Natural Disasters Inter-Action Pattern at Central Level.

Committees at National Level

Working of various other committees at the national level for disaster management is discussed in the following paras.

Cabinet Committee

The cabinet may set up a committee for effective implementation of relief measures in the wake of natural disaster. The secretary in the ministry of agriculture acts as the Secretary of this committee. In the absence of such a committee, all matters related to the relief shall be reported to the cabinet secretary.

National Crisis Management Committee (NCMC)

Under the chairmanship of cabinet secretary, the NCMC has been constituted in the cabinet secretariat. The other members of this committee include the secretary to prime minister, secretaries of ministry of home affairs, defence, research and analysis wing and agriculture and co-operation along with Director, Intelligence Bureau and an officer of cabinet secretariat. The NCMC gives direction to the crises management group as and when deemed necessary.

Crisis Management Group (CMG)

A group under the chairmanship of the Central Relief Commissioner, comprising senior officers drawn from various ministries and other concerned departments, reviews every year contingency plan formulated by central ministries/ departments. It reviews various measures required for dealing with a natural disaster, and coordinates activities of the central ministries and the State governments pertaining to disaster preparedness and relief and obtains information from nodal officers on measures relating to the above. The joint secretary (NDM) and Additional Central Relief Commissioner is the convenor of CMG. The CMG meets every six months.

Financial Arrangements

The centre plays a major role as far as mobilization of financial resources are concerned. The policy and arrangement for financing state governments to provide relief and rehabilitation measures in areas affected by natural calamities are governed by the recommendations of the finance commissions on the subject made from time to time. The scheme in force for the period 1995-2000 is based on the recommendations of the Tenth Finance Commission. Under the present scheme, a Calamity Relief Fund (CRF) has been constituted for each state with contribution from the Central and State Governments to undertake relief and rehabilitation measures. The annual allocations of the CRF to the various states are based on their trend of expenditure on natural calamities during the past ten years. The central share of CRF is released to the state governments in four equal quarterly instalments. As recommended by the Tenth Finance Commission, a committee of experts and representatives of the states has drawn up a list of items, expenditure on which alone will be chargeable to the CRF. A state level committee headed by the chief secretary decides the norms of assistance under each of the approved schemes. The norms so fixed could be modified by the Ministry of Agriculture, if these are significantly out of line.

In addition to the CRF, a National Fund for Calamity Relief (NFCR) has also been constituted to deal with calamities of rare severity. NFCR is available with the Government of India with an allocation of Rs 700 crore for the period 1995-2000. The fund is managed by the National Calamity Relief Committee, which is a sub-committee of the National Development Council, headed by the union agriculture minister. In normal circumstances, the state governments are required to undertake relief and rehabilitation measures utilizing the annual CRF allocations. They can, however, seek additional assistance from the NFCR in the event of calamity of rare severity.

Administrative Structure at State Level

As pointed out earlier, the central government only supplements the efforts of the state governments. The state governments are autonomous in organizing relief operations in the event of natural disaster and also long-term preparedness/rehabilitation measures.

The states have Relief Commissioners, who are in charge of the relief measures in the wake of natural disasters in their respective states. In the absence of the Relief Commissioner, the Chief Secretary or an officer nominated by him is in overall charge of the relief operations in the concerned State.

The Chief Secretary is the head of the State Administration. The state headquarters have, in addition, a number of Secretaries who head the various departments handling specific subjects under the overall supervision and coordination of the Chief Secretary. At the level of the state government, natural disasters are usually the responsibility of the revenue department or the relief department. While important policy decisions are taken at the state headquarters by the cabinet of the state headed by the chief minister, day-to-day decisions involving policy matters are taken or exercised by the secretary in the department.

States Crisis Management Group

There is a State Crisis Management Group (SCMG) under the chairmanship of Chief Secretary/Relief Commissioner. This group comprises senior officers from the departments of revenue/relief, home, civil supplies, power, irrigation, water supply, panchayat (local self–government), agriculture, forests, rural development, health planning, public works and finance.

The SCMG is required to take into consideration the infrastructure and guidance received, from time to time, from Government of India and formulate action plans for dealing with different natural disasters.

It is also the duty of the Relief Commission of the state to establish an emergency operation centre as soon as a disaster situation develops. Besides having all updated information on forecasting and warning of disaster, the Centre would also be the contact point for the various concerned agencies.

Administrative Structure at District Level

States are further divided into districts, each headed by the District Collector (also known as the District Magistrate or Deputy Commissioner), who is the focal point at the district level for directing, supervising and monitoring relief measures for disaster and for preparation of district level plans.

The Collector exercises coordinating and supervisory powers over functionaries of all the departments at the district level. During actual operations for disaster mitigation or relief, the powers of the Collector are considerably enhanced, generally, by standing instructions or orders on the subject, or by specific Governments order, if so required. Sometimes, the administrative culture of the concerned state permits, although informally, the Collector to exercise higher powers in emergency situations and the decisions are later ratified by the competent authority.

A district is sub–divided into sub-divisions and *tehsils* or *talukas*. The head of a sub-division is called the Sub-Division Officer (SDO) while the head of a *tehsil* is generally known as the *tehsildar* (*talukdar* or *mamlatdar* in some states). Contact with the individual villages is through the village officer or *patwari* who has one or more villages in his charge. When a disaster is apprehended, the entire machinery of the district, including officers of technical and other departments, swings into action and maintains almost continuous contact with each village in the disaster threatened area. In the case of extensive disasters, like drought, contact is maintained over a short cycle of a few days.

The various measures undertaken by the district administration area are discussed in the following paras.

Contingency Plans

At the district level, the disaster relief plans are prepared which provide for specific tasks and agencies for their implementation in respect of areas in relation to different types of disasters.

A contingency plan for the district for different disasters is drawn up by the Collector/Deputy Commissioner and approved by the state government. The Collector/Deputy

Commissioner also coordinates and secures the input from the local defence forces unit in preparation of the contingency plans. These contingency plans lay down specific action points, key personnel and contact points relating to all aspects.

District Relief Committee

The relief measures are reviewed by the district level relief committee consisting of official and non-official members, including local legislators and members of parliament.

District Control Room

In the wake of natural disasters, a control room is set up in the district for day-to-day monitoring of the rescue and relief operations on a continuing basis.

Coordination

The Collector/Deputy Commissioner maintains close liaison with the central government authorities in the districts, namely, army, air force and navy, ministry of water resources, etc., who supplement the effort of the district administration in the rescue and relief operation.

The Collector/Deputy Commissioner also coordinates all voluntary efforts by mobilizing the non-government organisations capable of working in such situations.

The entire hierarchy, right from the central government (the department of agriculture and co-operation in the ministry of agriculture and irrigation) to the district level, and even the sub-divisional/*tehsil* level, is connected with a telecommunication system. The normal mode of telecommunications is overland telephone and telegraphy, but in times of stress and if there is breakdown of the overland system, radio communication is resorted to. The wireless network is generally run and maintained by the police organisation in the country.

Besides the district officials, a host of other bodies too supplement their efforts in disaster situation—particularly the armed forces and the non-government voluntary organisations.

The Role of the Armed Forces

The armed forces of the country have played a vital role

during disaster emergencies, providing prompt relief to the victims even in the most inaccessible and remote areas of the country. The organizational strength of the armed forces with their disciplined and systematized approach, and with their skills in technical and human resource management make them indispensable for such emergency situations.

Besides, when disasters are spread over large areas, it is usually beyond the capability of the administration to organize the relief activities, the armed forces are then called in to organize the relief measures.

Related to the efforts of the armed forces, are the civil defence and home guard organizations. These organizations are voluntary in nature and character and come in handy during emergency situations like natural disasters. A network of these is now found all over the country. Their aim—while not actually taking part in actual combat operations, like in army—is firstly to save lives, to minimize damage to property, and to maintain continuity of production. Thus, while disaster situations often lead to chaotic conditions where rescue and relief work is severely affected, these organizations are able to coordinate and support efforts in a disciplined manner, so that both the army and the district officials are able to carry out their respective activities efficiently.

The Role of Non-Government Voluntary Organizations

Emerging trends in managing natural disaster, have highlighted the role of Non-Governmental Organizations (NGOs) as one of the most effective alternative means of achieving an efficient communication link between the disaster management agencies and the affected community. Many different types of NGOs are already working at advocacy level as well as grassroots level. In typical disaster situations, they can be of help in preparedness, relief and rescue, rehabilitation and reconstruction, and also in monitoring and feedback.

The role of NGOs is a potential key element in disaster management. The NGOs operating at grassroots level, can provide a suitable alternative as they have an edge over governmental agencies for invoking community involvement. This is chiefly because, the NGO sector has strong linkages with the community base, and can exhibit great flexibility in procedural matters vis-a-vis the government.

Based on the identified types of NGOs and their capabilities, organized action of NGOs can be very useful in following activities in different stages of disaster management.

TABLE 1
ORGANIZED ACTIVITIES OF NGOS AT DIFFERENT STAGES OF DISASTER MANAGEMENT

Stage	*Activity*
Pre-Disaster	Awareness and information campaigns Training of local volunteers Advocacy and planning
During Disaster	Immediate rescue and first-aid, including psychological aid, supply of food, water, medicines, and other immediate need materials Ensuring sanitation and hygiene Damage assessment
Post-Disaster	Technical and material aid in reconstruction Assistance in seeking financial aid Monitoring

In the recent past, NGO sector has played a major role in strengthening the community to face the disasters. The trend is based on a long-term experience of the need of maximum self-reliance at the lowest level.

The Role of the Community

It has now been revealed that the community as an institution in itself is emerging as the most powerful in the entire mechanism of disaster administration. In the event of actual disasters, the community, if well aware of the preventive actions it is required to take, can substantially reduce the disaster damage. Awareness and training of the community is particularly useful in areas which are prone to frequent disasters.

It is quite heartening to note the laudable effort made in certain areas where communities have formed their own organizations which take right initiative in such situations. One such community based organization is the Village Task Force formed in villages of Andhra Pradesh by the Church Auxiliary for Social Action (CASA). The Village Task Force has been trained in emergency evacuation and relief within the village. It is elected by the people themselves and during disasters it serves as the nodal body at village level which has to mobilize resources for the community and disseminates necessary information passed on by outside agencies.

While the community as an effective institution, is yet to take shape in this country mainly due to low literacy levels and widespread poverty, considerable efforts are being made to form and strengthen community-based organizations at grassroots levels.

Research and Training Institutions

With an increase in the perception towards spreading a culture of prevention in the disaster management scenario, considerable emphasis is now being placed on research and development activities, in addition to capacity building of all personnel concerned with disaster management. In India, a number of research institutes are conducting active research in the field of disaster management. Valuable inputs in technical, social, economic as well as management areas of the field are being looked into.

Research activities are being coordinated by different ministries depending on the type and level of research. An important role is played by the universities too in this sector who, besides running programmes on disaster management, also serve as think-tanks for the government. Institutes spread geographically across the country have developed specializations in terms of particular regions where most of their research is concentrated and also in terms of particular disasters. Notable universities are the University of Roorkee, the Indian Institutes of Technology, and the Anna University.

The Department of Science (Ministry of Science and Technology), Government of India coordinates activities through a network of scientific institutes, for example, the Central Building Research Institute at Roorkee. The Ministry of Urban Development carries out research through Building Materials and Technology Promotion Council on subjects, such as appropriate building materials for disaster-prone areas. These institutes, besides providing technical assistance to implementing and engineering organizations also trains field level officers and other concerned role players.

The Ministry of Agriculture and Cooperation too has set up a National Centre for Disaster Management at IIPA to look after administrative training activities in the field of disaster management.

The National Centre for Disaster Management

The centre was established by Ministry of Agriculture in March, 1995 at the Indian Institute of Public Administration, New Delhi. The NCDM, besides gearing up the national, state and district level administrations to tackle natural disasters, also coordinates various research and training programmes and builds a data-base on natural disasters.

Conclusion

In disaster situations, a quick rescue and relief mission is inevitable. However, considerable damage can be minimised if adequate preparedness levels are achieved. Indeed, it has been noticed in the past, that as and when attention has been paid to adequate preparedness measures, the loss to life and property has been considerably reduced.

Preparedness measures, such as training of role players, including the community, development of advanced forecasting systems, effective communications, and above all, a sound national policy and a well-networked institutional structure involving government organizations, academic and research institutions, the armed forces and NGOs would greatly contribute to the overall disaster management of the region. Later, it would lead to the much needed change in the overall orientation from rescue and relief to preparedness.

REFERENCES

Ajay Kumar, "The Role of Government of India in Natural Disaster Response" (Mimeo), 1997.

Army Training Command, *Policy Approach and Role of Various Organisations for Disaster Management in India*, 1996.

Amir Ali Khan, Anshu Sharma and Manu Gupta, "Role of NGOs in Disaster Management in India" (Mimeo), 1996.

India, Ministry of Agriculture, Government of India, *Contingency Action Plan for Natural Calamities*, 1990, New Delhi: Manager of Publications, 1990.

India, Ministry of Agriculture, Natural Disaster Reduction—South Asian Regional Report, New Delhi, Government of India, 1994.

International Federation of Red Cross and Red Creseant Societies, *World Disaster Report, 1994*, Geneva, 1995.

Verma, B.K., "Health Care in Disaster Situations" (Mimeo), 1994.

Sharma, V.K., "Natural Disaster Management in India" (Mimeo), 1997.

United Nations, *Yokohama Strategy and Plan of Action for a Safer World—Guidelines for Natural Disaster Prevention, Preparedness and Mitigation.* New York: The United Nations, 1994.

4

Anthropology of Disaster Management: An Indian Perspective

SACHINDRA NARAYAN

Introduction

The term 'disaster' may be defined as an unexpected happening causing a huge loss of life and property. Major disasters may be defined as those causing at least one of three consequences which are as follows:

(i) Causing damage to more than 1 per cent of Gross National Product.

(ii) Causing deaths of more than 100 persons at a time and place.

(iii) Affecting more than 1 per cent of total population of an area.

According to another estimate during 1950-92 about 5 lakh deaths took place due to major disasters out of which 1 per cent in developed countries and 99 per cent in developing countries. Before 1950 the situation was quite different and at that time 30 per cent of total deaths took place in developed countries and 70 per cent in developing countries. These figures indicate the gravity of the situation and seriousness of the problem.

All said and done, the point remains as to how to prevent, predict and mitigate major disasters? So far through scientific and technological development the prevention of earthquakes and cyclones, floods, droughts, fires, etc., may be possible and predicted to some extent. There is no doubt that a proper planning and effective management can reduce the effects and hazards of disasters like earthquakes since it is not the earthquake itself but the defective buildings which cause loss of life and property.

In Tribal Development an important issue which deserves consideration in the context of Anthropology of Disaster Management is the bottlenecks of the development processes of the planned development.

The concept of development is illusive. To some it may mean change; (but all changes are not necessarily development) to others it may be alleviation of poverty and well-being. Still to some others 'development' represents an increase in the capacities of a society to organise for its own objective and to carry out its programmes more effectively. Some hold the Marxian conception. Thus, many of us speak of development with reference to 'social', 'cultural', 'political' and 'economic' with the qualifying connotation or adjective or of a complex amalgam of all these. However, our reference is to the tribal society and with their problems, the resolution of which is so-called tribal development.

Development is an important phenomenon of the contemporary world and it is one of the study of which anthropologists have a very clear contribution to make. Understanding the phenomenon is important, not only because its potential for good or for ill is great, but because understanding can make a difference. It concerns what people do at least as much as what happens to them, choice and decision are prominent, and not only on the developer's side. The understanding in terms of which people act is, therefore, particularly significant here. It calls for what Malinowaski called 'practical' and which may be also called Applied and Action Anthropology. To some its scope is wide, so as to encompass all anthropological research which has been helpful to government while others take a more restricted view. To achieve sustained development in a country, its people have to benefit and also feel that they have benefited. Its leader and people have to establish appropriate roles and equitable relations that are personally rewarding and socially accepted. They have to rework the system of their society and culture to cope with the new conditions, reconciling disparate sectors, establishing revised channels for conflict expression and conflict resolution, making relevant knowledge available to all social strata, linking their society with world society.

All plans for development have greater chances for success if the relevant cultural and social factors are integrated into the planning. That integration, however, should not add yet another extraneous load on already overburdened planners. Social and cultural considerations must be so presented that they are plainly appropriate to the problems at hand and are clearly useful for makers of development decisions. There is no gain from deluging planners with data they cannot deploy, with recommendations too wordy to be carefully read or too abstruse to be readily understood. There is, however, great potential gain in broadening development policies so that they include significant forces that have hitherto been largely overlooked (Mandelbaum, 1981).

All the social and behavioural sciences can be tapped for this purpose. Anthropologists have special resources to offer (Mandelbaum, 1978). Their emphasis on a holistic view disposes them to take into account the social matrix in which particular problems are embedded. Their practice of fieldwork directs attention to development as perceived from within, how the people understand, accept or reject introduced innovations (C.F. Srinivas, 1977; Wallmen, 1977). Anthropologists are also inclined to relate what they learn in the microview to the macroview, to some general perspective on the human career (c.f. Patch and McMorrow, 1977).

Seen in the longest human perspective, development is part of a series of cultural thresholds crossed by humankind. At each successive crossing people gain greater control over their environment and enrich their material circumstances, as they did when some learnt to produce their food through agriculture and herding rather than to depend only on hunting and gathering. Soon after came the great social invention of civilization with its characteristic components of specialization of work, cities, state organization, writing very recently, as human history runs, some groups learnt how to command vast amounts of energy through mechanical and industrial means. And just a few generations later there came the upsurge in science, together with the highly effective, cumulative applications of science. In making a transition, a people share certain similar consequences with others who have done so, but different groups have crossed these cultural thresholds at different times, in quite different ways, impelled by differing reasons (Eisenstadt, 1977). From the vantage of this long view, current development efforts make up a movement to enable all peoples to benefit from the newly opened cultural potentials. But it is not enough to take over more efficient tools and agricultural procedures or to import tourists and export labour. That may result in some quick economic growth, but does not necessarily lead to lasting development, to being able to maintain a continuous flow of the material benefits, to achieving social and personal rewards made possible by new technology. If a people are to maintain higher productivity, they must also establish an appropriate social and cultural infrastructure for such development (Uphoff and Ilchman, 1972; Belshaw, 1972). That infrastructure includes adapted, revised institutions, associations, education, roles rewards, values. Social capital has to be built no less than physical capital (Mandelbaum, 1981).

There is no one road to development and certainly not the identical sequence traversed by countries now deemed to be developed. Whatever course is urged or coerced by planners and political leaders, each major group within a nation, eventually judges what the purpose of development is for them, and for whom the development bells toll. The outcome of any model of development depends ultimately on the effectiveness of their participation (De Kadt, 1974; Eisenstadt, 1977).

It is true that before other measures for development can be effective, certain basic conditions must prevail. People cannot do much construction for the future if many of them are struggling for more subsistence survival. Nor can development programmes take shape if a state is torn with turmoil, its land more the scene of battles than of building. But given such basic requirements, people do respond effectively to programmes for development if the programmes are presented in terms they can understand and accept. (Mandelbaum, 1981). When the people of a country become assured that their basic material needs are reasonably well available, then their aspirations for development are likely to turn to the quality of their lives. This concept includes a great many components that are not always mutually compatible or strictly logical. But a leading element is their shared idea that they are entitled to feel self-reliant, autonomous, worthy (or superior) as a people (Wallmans, 1977).

There is a growing number of people in many nations both in the more and in the less affluent, who realize that a satisfactory quality of life does not necessarily depend on over-increasing economic growth. Development, it is true, must first of all establish reliable provisions of the basic necessities for a physically secured life. But development processes do not stop there (Mandelbaum, 1981).

Anthropologists now have more opportunity than before to contribute to development. Their own ethical and procedural problems in the field have been sufficiently arised to permit such work to proceed at a fast pace. Planners and administrators are coming to realize that their previous models have slighted some critical elements, namely the cultures and societies of the people whom and on whom development plans were enacted (cf. World Bank, 1978: 33-42). Anthropologists not only view development problems from the perspective of the people, they also try to understand particular projects as parts of a larger system. And very frequently, it is the system of social relations and cultural understandings that is critical for the success or failure of projects. For, as we now recognize, development is not only the adaptation of advanced technology and economic programming, nor is it just another term for change. Development consists of purposive efforts by a people, led by public figures and planners, to organize themselves in new technical, cultural, and social ways. These are ways that will enable them to achieve the style and quality of life which they aspire. When their aspirations shift, the direction of development efforts much shift accordingly. (Mandelbaum,

1981). Tribal development consists of deliberate efforts by the tribals along with the planners, anthropologists and the elite groups to orient them towards the new cultural and social ways of life and actions. More adoption of new cultural and social ways of life and actions by the tribals is no longer a tribal development. When the tribals feel that the quality of life to which they aspire is in fact achieved, we may have a claim for tribal development. It may sound a dream of a Utopian society and seem even "impossible" to some of us to attain the level. The truth lies in the finding out how to approach the basic problems of the tribals and which gaps have held up the developmental process. It necessarily calls for the strategies to improve the prevailing affairs. Over the years since planning began, we have been working out strategies to improve the socio-economic conditions of weaker sections and development for the vulnerable groups. The poor, weaker, peasantry and slum dwellers were the pet subject of discussion for planners, professors and politicians until very recently. Out of gross vacillation or the inability to deal effectively with their problems, the ethos of our national feelings seems to have shifted very recently towards, the dearest of our weaker section namely the 'Scheduled Tribes'.

India is one of the few nations of the world noted for its tribal concentration. According to the 1981 census, the tribals in India account for 7.18 per cent of the total population. About 80 per cent of them live in remote forest areas and hill tracks without any access to modern socio-economic inputs.

Although there are ethnographic variations in terms of their 'anthropological identity', most tribals share certain characteristics: nature of rurality, speciality of illiteracy, economic backwardness and social deprivation. Their standard of living, judged by the standard measures of income position, calorie-intake, nutritional norms, educational standards and 'Physical Quality Life Index' (PQLI), does not fit anywhere within the scope and ambit of the Planning Commission's stylized standards. The employment problem of these communities can–not be discussed in isolation, for most of them are unemployed and a very few are engaged in traditional occupations. Their earnings, apart from the monetary angle, do not even conform to the barest minimum necessary for their sustenance. The expert definitions of the 'poverty line' or 'poverty gap' for these groups have yet to be defined or redefined.

Although articles 15(4), 46, 244 (i) and 339 of the Indian Constitution speak of special provisions meant for the administration and control of scheduled areas and tribals therein, for their welfare and protection, except for commissions and Reports, the executive power at the action level has done practically nothing to improve their socio-economic conditions. Of course, many heroic explanations have been advanced for their failures, but these do not seem to point out the culpability of tribal welfare departments and their protectors, just as the Harijans (The sons of God) referred to in the special provisions of our Constitution have become a 'sweet means' of exploitation for all who are concerned and connected with their welfare or ill-fare.

Even after three decades of independence, the tribals continue to remain aloof from the general prosperity of the nation and are still in the lowest strata of society. Their way of living is a challenge to modern civilization. They have been subjected to various types of exploitation for generations and their life is characterized by servitude, poverty and misery. Generally speaking, they are still under the clutches of their century old traditions and inimical customs. They are in the firm grip of a subsistence economy and indebtedness is the average hallmark of tribal existence in India.

The origin of the present day Integrated Tribal Development Projects (ITDP) can be traced back to 1950, when the Government of India initiated the National Extension Schemes (NES) in 1951, with the intension of intensifying the block level development activities to raise the general standard of living of the weaker sections. When the Block level activities became a blockade to the development of the weaker sections therein, a new scheme was reinstated in the name of the Tribal Development Block (TDB) in 1962. These blocks were able to initiate some efforts on the social welfare front of tribals. However, since these programmes were patterned after the development efforts attempted in the earlier periods, they turned out to be not in tune with the tribal context and culture.

But, the experiment over a periods of ten years or more proved that the emancipation of tribal communities was a complex process with serious socio-political and economic implications. The powerful feudal and vested economic interests, therefore, had to be fought against and new modes of role relations had to be established to ensure tribal claims.

These sporadic and isolated attempts could have only nominal impact on the welfare of the tribals. When it was found that the agencies created and appointed for tribal development were unqualified and ill-equipped to restrain the exploitation by powerful local forces, the Integrated Area Development Programme (IADP) was baptized in 1972 by the special convocation of the Tribal Development Department of the Ministry of Home Affairs with the consultation of various state level tribal development agencies. But, following the same line of experience as over the preceding years has proved that without developing the tribals therein cannot succeed. Yet, all of this seems to have got concealed in the new label of Sub-plan Scheme for Tribal Development (SSTD) in 1976 without defining the area coverage and plan objectives.

The new sub-plan under the main plan (of State and Union Government) started functioning in almost all states under the new name of Integrated Tribal Development Projects (ITDP) without 'project officials' to control, direct and manage the development activities of the various State and Union Government Departments. According to the new strategy, Area Sub–Plans comprising several projects are prepared for each such 'sub-plan area'. For each one of these projects, IADP focusing attention on the specific problems of the tribal people in that area has been formulated.

Consistent with the norms and directives of concerned departments, the Pilot Report, Preliminary Report, Primary Report, Pre-revised First Draft Report, Revised Confidential Report and Final Reports (strictly confidential and official) were prepared in all States. The State Planning Boards and Tribal Welfare Departments were entrusted with the task of preparing periodic reviews and studies on 'specific problem oriented tribal development issues'. Inspired by the heavy budget allocation for tribal development, the experts in the field were eager to conduct national and international seminars and conferences at the cost of the half appeased starving tribals.

'Action-oriented' researches were held under the expert guidance of eminent scholars in the field weeded to tribal life and dedicated to the welfare of the weaker sections of society. Resultantly, the volume of 'Reports' increased at an alarming pace along with the number of Institutes and 'Directors', Joint Directors, Deputy Directors, Additional Directors, Assistant Directors, Acting Directors and Special Executive Directors. But at the end of it all, the truth is sad indeed for the only comment that can be made is: 'poor are my tribals, rich are their protectors'. This is a fact that, the more the plans, the more are the tribals moving from 'poverty to absolute pauperism'. What they needed is not expert seminars, comprehensive reports or directives from ministers and ministries, but a time bound solution to their century old socio-economic problems with which they are struggling. Nevertheless, credit does go to the planners for what they have planned, rather than for what they have been able to do.

It is a fact that in all ages those who think must act for and govern those who toil for them. The people at the grass-roots level must feel proud of their more fortunate countrymen whose vision and learning can be of benefit to the more unfortunate masses. But the most distressing fact of our present day nationalism is that, instead of the elite and educated community representing the 'brain and consciousness of a nation', as the legitimate spokesmen of the illiterate masses-their dream, the custodians of their interest we have become actually anxious to exploit whenever and wherever possible.

Now we are aliens within our own national boundaries, strangers to each other and even to our own people. The ideas and beliefs of the nation are not shared by the masses or the people at the lower rung of the ladder, but only by a small class of affluent few for whom there is nothing more appealing than acquisition at any cost. They are clear about their own ends but not the means, thus shattering the fond dreams of the destitute millions who recoil with horror and dismay at what is generated by the liberal leaders of our political economy.

We are taught to be obedient to the 'law of the land' but not to be against the power of the few. We are taught that the 'law will take care of us', but not 'who will take care of the law' the 'masses or the mightly few'. If the achievement of political freedom is a proven historical and necessary event, the achievement of economic freedom is the natural right of every human being, a matter of the utmost urgency.

The genuine question that arises now is: should the government of the country be left to the elected representatives of the minority (in the factual sense) of their own party without any ideology to represent the masses. Should it be reduced to the level of street demonstrations and conspiratorial meeting? Even then, the masses are supreme. They must be trusted to define their economic objectives and to work for their strategies of development. The theories and models must become relevant to their needs and not become objects for 'soap bubble oratory', we must test our development theories so that we do not degenerate into a twentieth century off shoot of nineteenth century imperial legalits.

When social thinking is tandy and parochial, the power structure tends to keep an ambivalent attitude to institutional changes. This fact is evident in many fields of the development process in India. Thus, the social thinkers always become the worst enemies of a society which lives on the wages of exploitation. Pretence of action is worse than inaction. Inaction generates resistance and Pretence distrust. Thus, there is a fundamental difference between organized resistance and organized distrust. Both lead to conflict. But the latter invariably introduces an element of perversity. When programmes of development are initiated without certain institutional changes, one of the inevitable outcomes to begin with, is the strengthening of already entrenched social interests. This is what is happening in the case of tribal development in India. It is a game without rules. The brave words of the Planning Commission, except for sentimental potentialities, have failed to come to grips with the entrenched interests of tribal planners and protectors.

The party in power was unable to create any new and more effective instrument for the implementation of its social and economic policies than 'the crushing bureaucratic machinery' which has proved unsuitable beyond all doubt. In this context, advocacy of radical policies at the highest level of plan action does not get translated into fact. In fact, as policy declarations become more radical, the gap between the preaching and the practice becomes strikingly evident. So it is wiser to retreat to 'realistic plans rather than radical phraseology to which partymen are heroically accustomed. Therefore, it is not surprising that the present mode of development which has been stimulated over the years can only meet with failure.

The positive discrimination policy of the state on behalf of the disadvantaged groups and weaker sections of the society is the most effective way to help the tribals and weaker sections enter the modern mainstream. However, the quasi-structural frame, when linked with abstract development theories with the inbuilt institutional flavour, can only thwart the various measures for poverty eradication. The feasibility of measures of development through the superimposition of democratic institutions on a non-egalitarian social structure, is questionable; it stems from cynical and quacks, really, who believe in the self-percolation effect of the benefits of development towards the lower strata of the society. Such practice based on abstract theories has proved that well intentioned state intervention often ends up in accomplishing the very opposite of the objectives laid out in the plans and proposals. Any number of solutions to the problem of economic development of weaker sections in areas perennially handicapped by basic infrastructural constraints, coupled with gross financial misuse, organizational impotence, incorrect priorities and faulty identification processes will only help to aggravate the socio-economic tension which prevails within the backward tribal regions. Finally, the eruption of violence and bloodshed, in whatever form that we see in India, is not an accident but the inevitable outcome of the development experience.

Over the last three decades now, we have been planning, doing research and making policies for positive state intervention towards the most obviously disadvantaged groups in the society. But, by and large, the sad truth prevails that, by now the lack of political will has been amply demonstrated and gaps exist between the policy and the legislations, between the law and its implementation. Perhaps, there is no sphere of government action in our country which has shown such a deep hiatus between precept and practice as in the domain of planning for the weaker sections and socially deprived groups.

Despite all our integrated plan programmes and concerted efforts, the tribals still remain mostly disintegrated within our society. Unfortunately, planners are yet to define how to integrate and what to integrate, and why at all to integrate, if integration is a self-permeating process of economic development. But, it provokes us to think that if disintegration is the basic concealed objective under the disguise of integrated development, then nothing could be better done.

To bring the tribals into the mainstream of modern life, still a large gap has to be made up. But it is a reality that the tribals are much more socio-economically isolated and even if development is ensured, 'they are often dragged into subproletarian servitude by the reactionary forces of a society which lives on the wages of exploitation. The statutory reservations, discriminations, special provisions, guarantee of minimum needs, etc., as a means of social change is, no doubt, a welcome approach. This will bring about change in educational programmes, occupational mobility, cultural conditioning, redistribution and would also raise the overall competitive level of disadvantaged groups in what they are able to attain by their own effort and means.

No doubt, schemes and special provisions are obviously a help towards this end, but in the absence of comprehensive remedial measures to check the filteration processes of exploitative organs, they can only lead to social conflict and structural dislocation within already wounded social patterns. The reality is that the tribal plans look elegant and egalitarian, in appearance but the conspired practise makes the approach shabby and inegalitarian, as now the areas of elite catchment have widened to enlightened towns of 'integrated social groups'.

Most alarming of all, the special provisions have so far only ensured representation for the people who are in the power structure, who help to perpetuate the stratification in the social organizations. What is fundamentally wrong with the tribal development programme is a lack of awareness of the social dimensions, and the stunted vision on what needs to be done and how. So, the tribal development strategy calls for a change and reshuffle in the administrative structure towards those on whose behalf it is supposed to function. Otherwise, the proposals can only buttress social fragmentation. So the existing measures to improve the socio-economic condition of tribals must dissolve into a cohesive whole of the society of which the whole is larger than the sum of its part. But the question is, how to dissolve and what are the norms of division. Even otherwise, the virtual exclusion of wider objectives and substitution of temporary devices is only a conditional measure which makes the returns negative through short-sighted and misconceived policies which are objectively questionable and practically refutable (Verghese, V. Alexander, 1983).

Sometimes, the uncertainty of consequences of change among the tribals also block the developmental processes meant for them. They would rather go through a life which is known or familiar, than make a change where the consequences are uncertain. Fear of failure in the new ventures or new roles may deter them from taking advantage of the whatever little new opportunities provided to them. However, it does not mean that they do not like to live and lead the changed way of life, but the element of fairness sometimes resist the development process. An attempt towards the solution of the issues of why to approach and what to approach, may facilitate the tribal development process.

Moreover, a study covering about eleven countries, revealed some interesting trends in the context of social structures. Those who held positions in the centre (the top) were 'open minded' but sceptical, they possessed all the intellectual means for reconsidering their strategy, but they were not willing to introduce or accept major changes especially if those endangered their position. On the other hand, it was found that those at the periphery (bottom) were dogmatic, less educated, dissatisfied with their situation but without the initiative to change it, often not even aware of their own interest but eagerly advocating changes which they assumed would imply a development for the better. The 'top' predicted developments and achievements for which they did not show enthusiasm whereas those at the 'bottom' expressed their hopes for what they did not really believe would happen.

The 'top' who are close to the instruments of communication and decision making would be the ones to take initiatives, to plan and appear to be effectively in charge of what had to be done to meet the future. At the same time, those at the 'bottom', convinced that their ideas would not be realised anyhow, would do little to promote them. What they did would matter little anyhow, so long as they did it only at the individual level. One of the major stumbling blocks in the way of united action by those at the bottom is that while they do have quite a bit of change-oriented, thinking, it is rarely that the same idea prevails throughout those who constitute the periphery.

These are some observations based on a study across eleven nations which hold true in most of the hierarchical structures. In this context, any socio-economic change planned for groups occupying positions which are economically, socially, or both, vulnerable should take into account their feelings, their attitudes and the role of the structures—social, cultural, political, administrative—in shaping and reinforcing them. Therefore, improvements sought to be brought about among disadvantaged groups of people should not only take measures to unsettle the existing social structure but also modify the attitudes reflecting the dictates of that social structure (Muthayya, B.C. 1983).

Lack of interest in the tribal development by the administrative and executive personnel have also held up the developmental processes to a great extent along with lack of proper training to the administrative personnels, meant to implement the ambitious tribal development. No doubt, statistics tell us an impressive story of tribal development. Thus, each five-year plan allocation in respect of their preceeding one reveals an increase in the outlay and the fifth plan allotment of a sum of Rs. 1182 crore marked a phenomenal increase from earlier plan outlays. But an increase in the allocation of the outlays is no longer, a real achievement in the field of tribal development. And it may be remarked in the words of Adelmann and Morris that "hundreds of millions of disparately poor throughout the world have been hurt rather than helped by economic development". We often identify the tribal development with that of the economic development. We often assume that without economic development, the real tribal development cannot be achieved. No doubt, we cannot expect too much of the success of developmental schemes of the tribals when the basic needs are not assured to them. But it happens so that in doing it, we overemphasize the economic development as if the tribal development is wedded to the economists and divorced from anthropologists. In absence of social and cultural heritage of the tribal population, the schemes result into failure. It is not seriously taken into account both by the public and bureaucracy because of the fact that government schemes need not always succeed.

Moreover, the developmental programmes meant for the tribals are uniformly planned not keeping in mind the fact that there is a differential development among the tribals themselves and consequently of their needs. It may be observed that there is a well-marked differential development among those tribes who have adopted or are practising Christianity and those who are non-Christian. It may be added here again that the tribals who are still primitive or have dwellings on the hill, forests, and are not much in contact with the forces and agents of change of the plains, still show a poor state of affairs in contrast to the tribes which are on plains and to those who are exposed to the forces of industrialization and urbanization. It is evident from these facts that the developmental plans for the tribals should have a wide range of variability and should be formulated accordingly. Thus, the uniformity in the frames of plans, being away from the needs of a particular tribal community and its differentiation from the needs of another particular tribal group has also resulted in their failure. What it requires is not a separate plan for each tribal group, a long agenda, but must be in conformity with the classificatory tribal communities.

When we look at the tribal development in the state of Bihar, we are soon confronted with the sad picture that emerges even after a concerted effort made in the last 30 years of planning. It is still an experiment in the field, the cause and effect relationship remains to be inhibitory and inferences are far ahead to be drawn.

Studies conducted recently to examine the tribal participation in the developmental schemes through the institution of Panchayati Raj in the four Blocks of Ranchi district, reveal an increased participation. The latter is of utmost importance for the successful implementation of the developmental schemes meant for them. The figure that we have well explains the developmental efforts of the tribals for whom the developmental schemes are meant, but the stray cases cannot take the plaçe of generalizations. Moreover, the fruits of the project are taken by the non-tribals as the study reveals instead of the tribals.

Studies conducted on the Sauria Paharia of Bihar reveal a distressing picture. The tribe is facing extinction but no tangible solution has come up uptil now. The bureaucratic display of development achievement is a misnomer and bleak. There should be a close understanding between the implementing officials and the poor tribals in order to attain the goal of real development. There should be no gap between the officials and the tribals. Sometimes the tribal elite acts as a 'mediator' between the tribals and the officials, the bulk of the fruits of the schemes go in the share of the so-called elite group rather than those who really deserve it. Moreover, there should be a close understanding between the economists and anthropologists not at the planning level but also up to the evaluation stage. Such a wedding is not only inevitable but also realistic in the sense of improving in present state of affairs. A training to the officials for a fixed period is no longer a parameter to the fact that he/she has become competent enough to undertake the project and its success is imminent. A coach of class and an operation in the field are two distinct identities and cannot replace or clash but rather reinforce each other. The *symbiosis* can be of immense value for the effective launching of the schemes and its success is the objective before us to improve their lot.

The cooperative credit movement was started to get the farmers out of the clutches of the money lenders. Now the problem is how to get the cooperative movement out of the 'clutches' of the vested interests. It seems nobody has a solution to this. Panchayati Raj was introduced with a view to increase people's participation in development efforts. The basic idea was to get the development activities out of the 'clutches' of bureaucracy. Now, the problem is how to keep local bodies out of the 'clutches' of the local power-oriented politicians.

In short, the obvious conclusion is that the failure to improve the lot of the tribals in the tribal areas, so far, has been the result of a complex interplay of economic and political forces and many maladies in the administrative machinery. It seems the failure has been partly due to wrong policies and partly due to interest weakness in the political and economic institutions and administrative machinery, in addition to the faulty planning. All need careful investigations and corrections to realize the fruits of the tribal development in real sense. If we are really concerned for the development of the tribe then we have to think for their development in terms of their 'Felt' need and not in terms of their 'Assessed' need. What is being done till todate is that the needs are assessed by those who are strangers to them, which results into negative development. Data gathered from various departments of the State and central Government engaged in the development of tribes and reveal that approximately Rs. 3.75 lakh has been spent so far per square metre on their development. Density of population per square metre is two in tribal Bihar. Even if this amount would had been given as dole to each tribe, which comes to approximately Rs. 1.87 lakh it would have helped and reached each tribal.

An example of providing safe drinking water to Paharias without any cost but on which crores of rupees were spent and the result was zero, well explains the intentions and motive of the authorities involved. Prividing drinking water through experiment did not involve any expenditure as it was made available with the indigeneous materials. Bamboo is available in abundance among Sauria Paharia. Inner portion of the bamboo is hollow. One piece of bamboo was jointed with another and in this way 20 to 30 bamboos, sometimes more than this helped in bringing safe drinking water to the doorstep from the natural spring. These bamboos are periodically changed in order to keep the water safe. Likewise use of milk was also introduced in the community. These examples demonstrate that if the 'Felt Need' of the community is designed and implemented through participatory development then the chances of 'positive development' in the community is higher.

These days a good number of national and regional seminars are organized for the development of various state including Bihar and a good number of recommendations are being made. But the pre-condition for any development is the human behaviour and its management which is missing the 'participatory development' or the 'empowered development' is a development from within the community for which understanding of human feeling is a must probably here anthropologist have a great role to play.

Observations

Thus it is evident from the foregoing discussions that the Anthropology of Disaster Management broadly discusses the Natural Disaster as well as the man made disaster. At the beginning of 21st century the anthropologists are more concerned with the man made disasters. Researches and development in science have minimized the occurrence of natural disasters but through planned development the occurrences of manmade disaster have maximized. Death of innocent people in explosions and bomb blasts, proxy wars, sex scandal of U.S.A. President, Bill Clinton, spread of HIV and AIDS, ethnic violence in Canada, etc. are a few glaring examples of manmade disasters. In course of time we learnt the art of controlling the natural disasters but we are yet to learn the management of disasters caused by man. Majority of disasters of 21st century will be due to human failure. The emotions, human feelings, fellow feelings, compassion, fear from God, etc., have evaporated and have been dried in human beings due to scientific and planned development. If anthropology has to survive it has to take care of such disasters and UNESCO has rightly declared the 21st Century as the century of Anthropology.

We must therefore stress at world level meetings of anthropologists that development is for mankind rather than mankind being there for development.

5

New Dimensions of Disaster

SHASHI B. SAHAI

Mankind has survived and lived with natural disasters right from the days of the mythical universal deluge. Floods, volcanic eruptions and earthquakes have plagued and devastated humanity since time immemorial. Recurring floods are believed to have contributed, among other factors, to the extinction of the flourishing Indus valley civilization of South Asia in ancient times. You can do nothing about shifting of tectonic plates beneath the oceans causing devastating earthquakes or lava simmering underneath the earth's crust to erupt violently. And if our astronomers are to be believed, our planet is facing the dire prospect of total annihilation by a Hailey comet striking it in less than one and a quarter century from now. The exact year of their dark prediction is 2116. Human endeavour in respect of such natural disasters, which are beyond human control and regulation, is limited to deep study, fact-finding and forewarning by natural scientists concerned. These are beyond the perview of social scientists.

There is another category of disasters facing humanity today which is very much in the agenda of social scientists. This is the category of man-made disasters which calls for earnest attention of researchers in humanities, if mankind has to be saved from much avoidable damage. Some of these are almost as deadly and certainly more frequent than natural disasters. As man approaches the 21st century he is more and more exposed to the threat of man-made disasters almost invariably resulting from mismatch between ever proliferating technological innovations and man's capacity to handle them. It is not meant to decry technological innovations in production of goods and services or call for a halt to revolutionary changes they entail in the affairs of human beings. Rapid technological advance is an irreversible process and, if anything, it is only going to accelerate in future. The objective behind any in-depth study of man-made disasters could only be to increase the awareness about the inherent dangers, which is lacking at present and evolve effective damage control policy.

Before talking about the strategy in abstract, some of the well-known and not so well-known flash points of disasters may be identified and dwelt upon. This study deals with two such flash points—environmental disaster, and industrial disaster. Some factual indicaters are being provided in respect of environmental disaster to highlight the dangers involved, which is meant to be only illustrative. Facts about the less known kind of industrial disasters have been derived largely from the Bhopal Gas Tragedy of India which was perhaps the worst industrial disaster of history.

Environmental Disaster

Global warming is the most important component of environmental disaster that mankind is facing today. Unprecedented increase in world population, coupled with even faster increase in economic activities is threatening to disrupt the finely balanced eco-system which sustains life on earth. In 1900 the world population was about 1.6 billion which rose to 2.5 billion by 1950. But during 40 years from 1950 to 1990, the world population more than doubled. What is more, world economic activity increased more than four times in the same period. The need to support more people and rapid technological advance to enable them to live better have been steadily eroding the fine ecological balance. Hyper industrialization is leading to abnormal rise in the level of CO_2 emissions—CFC's (Chlorofluro-carbons), acidified forests, polluted rivers, etc. This has such a disturbing effect on the eco-system that more of sun's radiant energy or heat gets trapped within the earth's atmosphere, as inside the glass of a green house. This results in warming up of not only the atmospheric gases but of everything else on earth.

At the same time, chemical emissions like CFC's are adding up to the harmful effects of solar radiation in another way. The Ozone layer, situated about 20 kilometres above the earth's surface, protects the earth from the harmful effects of sun's rays. Chemicals like CFC's widely in use in refrigeration, air-conditioning, etc., cause depletion of the Ozone layer, resulting in what has come to be known as 'Ozone hole'. The wider the 'Ozone hole', the greater the danger of sun's rays directly penetrating the earth's atmosphere unfiltered by the protective shield of ozone, resulting in serious consequences for global population.

Galloping population and even faster pace of industrialization are thus slowly but steadily leading to rise in earth's temperature through greenhouse effect and ozone depletion. This could prove to be disastrous for large chunks of inhabitants of our planet. It is estimated that average increase in global temperature in course of the last one hundred years was only to the extent of 0.3° celcius to 0.7° celcius. As against this insignificant rise, it is estimated that double the CO_2 emission levels, consequent upon accelerated population growth and industrialization, will produce an average temperature increase of between 1.5°celcius to 4.5°celcius by the middle of the 21st Century. One of the consequences of this abnormal increase in global warming could be perceptible rise in earth's sea levels. This would be inescapable because a warmer liquid has more volume than an equivalent mass of cold liquid.

In concrete terms, any significant rise in sea level during the 21st Century may spell disaster in many countries of the Third World. For instance, a one-metre rise in sea-level would submerge about 11.5 per cent of the land of Bangladesh containing a population of about 8.5 millions. Similar would be the fate of large populations residing on low-lying deltas in Egypt and China. A two-metre rise in sea-level would completely swallow up the Maldive islands, inhabited by about two hundred thousand people, as well as many atolls in the Pacific ocean.

Although the potential damage caused by global warming may be less severe in developed world, it cannot escape the disastrous consequences altogether. Low-lying regions of Louisiana, New Jersey, the Netherlands, etc., would remain vulnerable to varying degrees of devastations through rise in sea-levels. In the USA alone, a rise of one metre in the sea-level would devour up to eight thousand square miles of wet-lands and ten thousand square miles of dryland. The vintage city of Venice and many other towns and habitations located near water's edge would be seriously threatened.

Industrial Disaster

While there is growing awareness about the threat of environmental disaster looming large over the world, not much is known about the ever increasing dangers of industrial disasters. As the process and pace of industrialization goes on accelerating the world over, with poor countries emulating and vying with their richer counterparts in the race towards greater and yet greater industrialization, the threat of industrial disasters is ever widening across the board. Major and minor industrial disasters are taking place regularly across the world but these are not so well-known. Everybody is interested in blanking these off the public gaze, the corporations, governments and the entire network of institutions and people involved in the concerned industries, for their own reasons. In any case, the common people tend to dismiss industrial disasters as no more than accidents or normal hazards associated with any trade or industry. But taken together, they constitute a serious threat to human life with grim prospect of multiplying as the process of industrialization intensifies in the approaching century.

A few samples of industrial accidents taking considerable toll of human lives across the world are given below:

In 1942, a coal dust explosion at Honkaiko colliery in China left 1572 dead on the spot.

In 1947, a Fertilizer ship explosion off Texas city in USA killed 561 persons.

In 1956, 1100 died in a dynamite truck explosion in Cali, Columbia.

In 1975, 433 miners perished in a coal mine disaster in Chasnala colliery in India.

In 1979, an accident in the biological and chemical warfare plant at Novosibirsk in erstwhile Soviet Union took 300 lives.

In November 1984, natural gas explosion at Pomex plant in Mexico city left at least 452 dead and 4258 injured; 31,000 residents of the area had to be evacuated.

The industrial disaster that dwarfed all others in the scale of devastation occurred at the city of Bhopal in central India in early December 1984. The event which has left many in the city permanently disabled, apart from thousands who were directly consumed by it, was summed by a leading fortnightly, "India Today" dated 31 December, 1984 as follows:

"The night of December 2/3, a night that Bhopal and its 800,000 citizens can never forget. A Monday of macabre death, a killer cloud of gas that silently settled on an unsuspecting city and converted a pleasant, mild winter's night into a nightmare of misery, panic, sickness and, for at least 2500 people, babies and children, fathers and mothers, siblings and grandparents, a slow, painful, unnecessary snuffing out of life. That it was the worst ever industrial accident in history, taking an unprecedented and still unaccounted death toll and leaving no fewer than 50,000 affected, was quickly dwarfed by the tidal wave of human suffering that spread quickly across the city like the poison cloud that caused it.

"Mithyl isocyanite (MIC) a product that few in Bhopal knew even existed, which Union Carbide, its makers describe in the manuals as 'an extraordinarily hazardous chemical,' a poison against which 'stringent precautions must be observed to eliminate any possibility of human contact', yet it was this lethal substance, a highly volatile chemical that is used by Union Carbide to manufacture pesticide that vaporised silently into Bhopal's night air".

The tragedy was caused by both systems and human failures. The systems that failed were (a) vent gas scrubber, (b) flare tower, (c) water curtain, (d) refrigeration system and

(e) spare tank. Even if some of the systems failed, the plant staff could have adopted the laid down measures to render most of the MIC escaping into the air harmless, which they failed to do. As a result, more than a hundred thousand people living in the vicinity of the factory were exposed to MIC in varying degrees. Around sixteen thousand animals perished immediately.

As the poison gas leaked out of the chemical plant, gradually bringing under its sway a 40 square kilometre area, men, women and children started dying of asphyxiation. The immediate body count put the figure of the dead at 3000, even as more dead bodies were being discovered everyday even a week after the disaster. Even according to the conservative official estimates, no less than one-fourth of the city's population of about eight hundred thousand was affected by the deadly effect of the gas leak. Many were completely blinded, many had their eye-sight and hearing partially impaired and still others were maimed one way or the other. The scars of the disaster are still there on the face of Bhopal in the shape of numerous hapless inhabitants who have become handicapped for life in the prime of their youth. Bhopal has become a symbol of the magnitude and omnious dimensions of industrial disasters the world over.

Yet another disaster of grave magnitude occurred in Chernobyl nuclear plant in the erstwhile Soviet Union in 1986. There have been less serious accidents at nuclear plants in other countries which have generally been kept under the curtain of secrecy by the countries concerned for strategic reasons. But Chernobyl was too big a nuclear disaster to be hidden from world view. Hundreds perished instantly, though the exact tally would never be known, and thousands were maimed by radio activity. Huge expanses of land were rendered infertile for decades. As one observer put it, the poisonous wastes it left behind would have a life time far larger than any human culture has survived.

The range, sweep, scale and frequency of man-made disasters constitute a grim prospect for human well-being in the coming century. It is necessary for social scientists to give serious thought to the problems posed by man-made disasters. By all accounts, there is going to be no let up in the pace of population increase, technological advance and industrialization in the foreseeable future. With the poor and developing countries racing headlong to catch up with the developed ones, there is every possibility of industrialization increasing at a faster pace rather than slowing down, in the process, augmenting the range, ferocity and frequency of disasters. In the event, the only way out is to evolve a suitable strategy to contain and minimize the risks involved.

Human Audit

This would involve reorienting our attitude towards technological advance and industrialization. These are engines of development and essential for economic betterment of people particularly in the poor and developing countries. But in the race for economic development, latent risks of potential disasters cannot and should not be ignored. A bold new approach to the issue is called for. There should be a human audit of technological innovations and modes of industrialization before going ahead with these engines of growth. For instance, the desirability of launching upon chemical and nuclear projects should be examined with reference to the threat they pose to human life in the light of Bhopal and Chernobyl disasters. Human ingenuity is capable of evolving alternative modes of industrialization and tapping new energy sources which are safer or less prone to disaster.

As discussed earlier, hurtling to industrialisation through the carbon route is fraught with possibilities of environmental degradation, leading to global warming and attendant dangers to human life. The human cost involved must be weighed before rushing through such a course of economic development in developed and developing countries. Any such human audit would point to an alternative course, that is, a non-carbon path to industrialization in less developed countries which are seeking to industrialize fast and improve the economic conditions of their people. The developed countries too should evolve and increasingly take to such alternative modes of economic activity, not only to cut down the damage already done, but also to provide a model for the less developed. They are certainly in a better position to do that, being in the vanguard of technological advancement.

6

Disaster Management Under the British Raj A Case-Study of Famines in Bihar in the Late 18th Century

YUVARAJ D. PRASAD AND PRASANTA DUTTA

Disaster means an adverse or unfortunate event, a great and sudden misfortune or a calamity. In this sense, famine is also a calamity caused either by nature or man. Famine which means acute shortage of foodgrains was caused by natural calamities such as excess rainfall or absence of rain caused by flood and drought, operation of insects, pests, etc. It was also caused by purely human factors and by operation of historical and economic factors, such as wars, trade, depression, heavy taxation etc.[1]

Scarcity was caused by dryness of the climate or lack of rain and insufficiency of food respectively. Scarcity was also caused by the policy of economic drain which caused scarcities in respect of foodgrains, textile products, agricultural products, minerals, etc. Scarcity was more man-made in the sense that it was more the product of the colonial economic system.

Famine and scarcity cannot be separated. Both were restricted to limited localities and varied in intensity. Scarcities caused famines and vice versa. Thus, famines and scarcities in India meant in the words of W.C.A. Knowles, "a lock-out in the agricultural industry since agriculture is the main industry of the country and affects directly or indirectly, the whole social and economic life of Indian community".[2]

Famine was one of the most serious disasters that the people and the administration faced during the British Raj. The chapter seeks to study the famines of 1770, 1783 and 1787 in Bihar.[3] In this context an attempt has been made to study the causes and impact of such famines on the rural society in Bihar and also to assess the various measures undertaken by the government and private individuals to manage the disasters. Much work has been done on subsistence crisis in 18th century Bengal. But though Bihar formed an important part of the then Bengal Province, both economically and politically, the devastation of the 18th century subsistence crisis in Bihar has not received much attention of scholars. This study seeks to fill this gap.

Famine had been a very common feature since time immemorial. We find references to famines in India in the Rigveda, in which a prayer is offered to drive poverty and famine far from us. Though, a connected and complete account of all the famines which occurred in pre-British India is lacking, the available evidence suggests that in the earlier times a major famine occurred once in every fifty years.[4] From the beginning of the 11th century to the end of the 17th, there were fourteen great famines, almost all of which were confined to regions very much limited in area.[5] During October 1670 to November 1671, the Rajmahal area had been affected adversely. A graphic account of it has been left by Thomas Bowery and John Marshall of the East India Company then stationed at Patna.

From their remarks it appears that this famine was not due so much to failure of crops, as to administrative malpractices. In a sense it was a man-made famine. Though the previous year was dry, there were large quantities of rice in these areas. Evidently the available stocks were withheld and the markets were controlled by the officials. As it was Aurangzeb's region, Marshall attributes the famine principally to the Nawab's roguery. According to Marshall's description Hajipur and the entire areas from Mokamah to Patna had been devastated by the famine.[6]

Apart from this famine no famine occurred in Bihar in the 17th century. But in the second half of the 18th century Bihar witnessed three major famines in 1770, 1783 and 1787.

The Famines of Late 18th Century

The famine of 1770 was an "appalling spectre on the threshold of British rule in India".[7] Bihar, one of the richest and prosperous provinces of India, was first hit by this famine. It occurred partially due to the failure of the crops in December, 1768 and September, 1769, and greatly due to the lack of governance, administrative disorder, social insecurity, economic decline, abuse of private trade by the company servants and oppressive revenue collections. Administrative disorder and misgovernance were results of the Diwani. The Nawab became titular and the company divested itself from responsibility. The British Chief at Patna received the revenue from Raja Shitab Rai who acted as Naib Diwan and Naib Nazir. Such an arrangement was bound to fail.

The Nawab's officers who were immediately incharge of administration possessed neither character nor means to enforce decisions, and the British who commanded power and resources worried little as long as their revenue receipts continued unaffected. The result was that the Nazir exacted as much as they could from the peasants.

The Company's servants, on the other hand, advanced their private trade through native *gomasthas* who in the name of their masters forced the unhappy natives to buy and sell goods at arbitrary rates.[8] To remedy these evils, supervisors were appointed in Bengal in 1769 and Bihar districts in 1770. In Bihar supervisors appointed for Saran and Champaran, Sahabad, Tirhut, Rohtas, Purnea, Monghyr and Patna continued to be under the charge of the Chief of Patna. A few months later a controlling council of revenue was established at Patna for the whole of Bihar, and at Murshidabad for Bengal.[9]

But these proved to be half-hearted measures. The plan of supervision was only exploratory, not executive in nature. In point of ability and honesty, many of them lagged far behind expectations. But even those who were able and honest could not interpose and punish exactions. Whatever may have been the conduct of individuals, wrote Warren Hastings, the blame is not so much attributable to them as to the want of a principle of government, adequate to its substance, and a coercive power to enforce it".[10]

Clive was succeeded by Verelst as Governor of Bengal in 1767 and the condition worsened in his time. He had seen with his own eyes the revenue collectors oppressing the people and often reported to the Court of Directors. Corruption and oppression became rampant because of the desire of the collectors to make the collection as large as possible with a view to win the grace of their masters and to make their own fortunes.[11] Thus the economic condition of the *ryots* as well as of the Zamindars was becoming very deplorable as they had no capacity to face any scarcity or famine situation.

Another cause of the famine in Bihar in 1770 was a partial failure of crops in Bihar in December 1768 on account of the failure of rains. In the early months of 1769 there were high prices. But the September crop which was far less important than December harvest, was also scanty. The drought had its evil effect on the harvest. Mr. Rumbold, the Company's supervisor of Bihar in his letter to Verelst the Governor of Bengal, dated 29th November, 1768 informed him about the great drought that was prevailing over Bihar. He also informed him about the scarcity of grain from the beginning of the year 1769. In the month of August, rice was hardly to be found in the market. Distress became so acute that Rumbold and Shitab Rai could not walk publicly without being stopped in the streets by multitudes of hungry people.[12]

As Bihar was then a part of Bengal Presidency, the Maratha raids affected Bihar too. Prices of the articles were increasing day by day, which caused great distress to the people till the terrible famine of 1770 appeared as a great catastrophe.

Thus we see that famines occurred due to various factors. The main causes of the Indian famines, particularly the Bihar famine during 1770-1800 was the poverty of the people, heavy taxes, inadequate agricultural methods, the burden of a caste system containing largely number of unproductive people and British drain upon Indian resources have been offered as explanation of Indian poverty.[13]

The famine of 1770 was of different intensity in the various districts of Bihar. The districts worst affected were Purneas. Patna, Bhagalpur, Rajmahal, Saran and Champaran, Sahabad and Rohtas, Monghyr, Tirhut, etc.

The famine of 1783, which followed that of 1770 was most devastating for the inhabitants of Bihar. It was much more widespread and severe and occurred due to lack of seasonal rainfall.[14] The Hathiya rain had failed in the autumn of 1782. The prices of necessary articles were rising. Soon after this, in 1783 the rain ceased before the last week of August, by the end of September the price of rice rose to 20 seers for the rupee, and it was evident, when we see the previous price list of the grain that serious scarcity was impending.

Actually no rain had fallen for months in any part of Bihar excepting Tirhut, and although the lands had been perhaps better cultivated than in the earlier year, the labours of *ryots* had been rendered useless for the want of rain, without which the grain could not be sown.[15]

Besides the failure of rain, the excessive revenue assessment, the various rebellions against East India Company Government and the corruption prevailing in the present system of governing bodies such as Collectors, Naibs, Aumils, Zamindars, etc., all combined to make 1783 a year of intense sufferings. However, the changes introduced by Warren Hastings, in the revenue administration in 1781 further intensified the problems. As an administrator his main outlook was to collect more and more revenue. This attitude had a bad effect on the masses. Thus the heavy assessment of revenue collected by corrupt officials had given more pain to *ryots*. Many of them decided to cultivate their lands.

Export of grain from Bihar to other provinces, for example to Madras for feeding the people including sepoys or troops led to shortage of foodgrains. In 1782-83 the want of Madras rose to the pitch of severe famine. Throughout 1783 the necessities of Madras continued. The Bengal Council then rightly observed. "When the enemy was at their walls and by his ravages in every part of the adjacent country had destroyed the cattle and reduced the inhabitants of the most pressing difficulty to obtain the most common necessaries of life."[16]

It was in September and October 1783 that Bihar was in the grip of acute shortage of rain and extreme drought. In the latter half of September, all the Collectors in Bihar, as well as the Officer in-Charge of Purnea sent very alarming report. Though a few showers of Tirhut induced the Collector of that district to write more hopefully, in the beginning of October his hopes were disappointed and the later rain crop certainly failed very generally in all parts of the province. In October 1783 the Governor General made the vivid report of the terrible famine in this province, as well as in the whole of the country.[17]

Thus, the above mentioned causes made the living of the inhabitants of Bihar in 1783 extremely difficult. The scarcity of foodgrain was severely felt at this time and people perished in large numbers due to devastations and starvation. However, the loss of one year's harvest could not have caused such a severe scarcity in 1783, if the heavy revenue assessments collected by different types of collectors, private trade, the system of hoarding the grain, etc., were not prevalent in the society.

In 1787 the famine and horror of 1783 was repeated again. The scarcity caused by a severe flood made the situation grim and destroyed many lives. From the beginning to the end of the season, rains, floods and storms continued unabated.

From several of the reports of the Collectors it appears that the rains commenced abnormally early and continued for months. It stated that Bihar, from the beginning of June to the latter half of July had constant rains which made cultivations impossible. Terrible damage had been done in this province, the inhabitants were driven from their homes, the cattle drowned, and general alarm and scarcity prevailed. There was a break in the rain and some fine weather towards the end of July which gave some hopes of survival. But that was succeeded by fresh violent inundations. At this, the collectors of Bihar pathetically remarked, "After three separate attempts to grow their lands, the *ryots* again find all their hopes vanished, and now the season is gone". In the end of September 1787 there were renewed account of great storms and inundation in Bihar doing immense damage.[18]

The crisis and conclusion of all these series of calamities occurred on 2nd November, 1787, when a cyclone of quite big intensity seemed to have swept across almost the whole of Bengal including the province of Bihar. By this disaster the late crops were destroyed in great measure over large parts of the country.[19]

The famine of 1787 was not as devastating as that of 1783 for the people of Bihar. But within a short interval these two famines occurred one by one. While the people were recovering from 1783's devastation, another followed in 1787, which made the condition of the common people worst.

Thus, we see that the famines in Bihar during 1770 to 1800 were caused by various factors. But undoubtedly one common factor of all these famines was the abject poverty of the people. However, the apologists of British rule try to argue that the real cause of Indian poverty was not character of the exploitative political system, but the pressure of population, waste of money on festivals and feasts, the conservative character of the people, the idle front of Indian noble men, maintenance of idle Brahmins, early marriage, indolence and infrugality of peasants, oppressions of landlords, litigations, etc.[20] But such arguments only sidetrack the real issue. The density of population in most parts of India was far less than other countries and even its rate of increase was slower than in other parts of the world. The real problem, therefore was, not the increase in population, but that the return from land was not increasing and there were no other sources to supplement the income of the people. Over population was confined to restricted localities, which were dependent on their industrial, political or social importances. So Lovedy is correct in his conclusion that it is difficult to find evidence to prove that over population was an overall reality in India.[21]

One may partially accept the arguments put forward by the apologists of British rule that the conservative attitude of the Indians was responsible for the poverty, famine and scarcity in India. But that cannot be accepted as the sole factor of Indian poverty. The real causes for India's poverty were—foreign rule, ruin of Indian industries, the oppressive revenue system, heavy taxation and the defective judicial system which had given great power to moneylenders. The produce of the land was then not enough to meet the needs and requirement of the people and because of the lack of the local industries to provide alternative occupation, suffering was inevitable. All this facilitated the cultivation towards chronic indebtedness and compelled many of them to migrate to other states.

Relief Measure

Relief measures to tackle the famines in Bihar during 1770-1800 had been taken by the Company's administration and some private individuals. One such governmental measure was to reduce their expenses. They reduced the stipend of Naib Nazim by 10 lakh, they discontinued the allowance to the Resident in lieu of the Zamindars contribution of provisions, they directed Reja Khan to keep the stipends and allowances as arrears and ordered their Resident at the Darbar to withhold atleast 30 lakh of rupees from the tributes and other allowances.[22]

Another relief measure of the administration was keeping in store sufficient grain not only for the soldiers but also the famine stricken people. From the very beginning of the famine of 1770 in Bihar, attempts were made to procure grain from the kingdom of Shuja-ud-daulah and those districts of Bihar which were immune from famine. The grain thus procured was to be first collected in Patna and then to be sent to various military stations and factories in Bihar and Bengal. In one letter of Shuja-ud-daulah dated 25 June, 1770 he stated that fifty-nine boats had been despatched in all to Patna containing 18,200 mounds of grain and that thirty-two more boats would be sent in due course of time.[23]

Another measure which the Company's government took for the relief of the famine stricken people was remission and suspension of revenue during the famine. For example, the total collection for Purnea in the year 1769-70 were Rs. 11,90,476 but the remission granted was on Rs.19,084. In

Raj Mahal the net revenue was Rs. 2,84,982 and the remission granted was Rs. 80,000. However due to lack of records we do not find the correct amount of revenue remission.

The next step taken by the Company's Government for the relief was the grant of Takavi to the ryots from 11 April 1769 to the end of March 1770. In Bihar, Rs. 1,06,489 was advanced to the *ryots* in 1769-70 of this, Rs. 45,036 was realized the very next year. In 1770-71 the sum of Rs. 1,02,000 was distributed as Takavi.[24]

In that time of distress, the opulent section of the public extended their helping hands to the needy. In Purnea, the Faujdar and Diwan Devi Singh spent Rs.4000 and Rs.2000 respectively from their own money in distributing rice as charity. Raja Shitab Rai also set a noble example. He set apart a sum of Rs.30,000 and directed that boats and rowers of his household should bring regularly to Azimabad, three times a month, the grain purchased with that sum form Benaras.[25]

With the instruction received from the Home Government, the Company's administration of 1783 exercised a much more active involvement with the grain trade than in 1770. A Committee of Grain was at once appointed with full power to regulate all dealings in the articles and superintend the price distribution and sale of rice throughout the province. Its President, Thomas Graham Esq and the members of the Committee being put under the sacred oath to desire no advantage directly or indirectly from their trusts. The committee of grain was authorized to establish granaries at Patna and other places.[26] As a famine officer of Bihar, John Shore issued a proclamation by which he required merchants and zamindars to bring to sale all stored grains or face its confiscation. Merchants were warned of dire consequences if they failed to sell the grains at reasonable price.[27]

Shore also took the sensible step of removing the transit duties on grains and he cancelled the orders of the collections from Saran and Tirhut, who seeing the scarcity in Patna, had endeavoured to protect their own districts by forbidding exportation.

Sir George Campbell in his account of the famine of 1783 says, "It was decided that buildings of solid masonary should be constructed to serve the purpose of perpetual granaries to the two provinces—Bihar and Bengal, and the Chief Engineer prepared a plan for a circular building at Patna, which still stands (Golghar) as a monument of past resolutions, bearing its inscription "For the perpetual prevention of famines in India, but empty and disused". Thus, one result of Shore's recommendation was the building of the great granary, Golghar near Gandhi Maidan. Its creation was sanctioned in January 1784, and it was promptly built, but it had never been filled in anticipation of scarcity.[28]

John Shore as a famine officer in Bihar made his famous Settlement of 1783 to face the famine of 1783. The settlement expired in 1785. But it caused only a minor change from the previous year. This did not actually satisfy the general masses of the ryots. They had always been exploited by different kinds of taxes and collectors.

Though Bihar was not as much affected by the famine of 1787 as Bengal, still to face it, the collectors were instructed by Cornwallis in August 1788 for Decenial settlement which was made permanent in 1793. But the settlement failed to have the desired effects. Unrest prevailed in some Parganas of Bihar with disturbances breaking out in between Khalda and Tomar between 1789 and 1795. For non-payment of arrears of the revenue, the Pachet state was put up for sale in 1795. There was additional complication in the situation due to fresh Chuar insurrection in 1798-99 in the Pargana of Raipur, Ambikanagar, Manbhum and Birbhum.

Relief measures of the government and private charity in the Bihar famines between 1770 and 1800 were in no way adequate to meet the situation. The various relief measures of the government discussed earlier in the study during the crisis of 1770 proved to be a failure. One important reason was that servants and officers of the Company were corrupt. Takavi loans meant for the peasants never reached them in time. Quick realization of loans with interest proved a greater hardship for peasants. Justification offered for this type of corruption was the low pay of the officials. They had no fixed salary. Hence they were allowed to carry on private trade.

One immediate impact of the failure of relief measures was the rise in the prices of foodgrains. People suffered because they did not have enough money to buy foodgrains. Price rise and shortage strengthened the merchants greatly. It was they who dominated the entire grain market, hoarded grain, and the price rise that resulted due to their activities was the main source of profit during a period of shortage.

Famines of 1769-70, 1783 and 1787 also caused demographic changes, due to large-scale death and migration. Historians are divided over the number of mortality deaths, but the fact that a large number of deaths occurred has not been rejected by any historian. The fact remains that in the absence of statistical data of proper census one cannot reach any conclusion regarding the numbers. But mathematical accuracy in mortality rate due to famine and subsequent epidemic need not concern us too much. There is enough evidence to suggest that depopulation was enormous.

Though the extent, nature and direction of migration differed according to the intensity of the famines, it cannot be denied that after the famines the displaced were forced to migrate over long distances in search of food and employment. The people of Shahabad district migrated to Benaras where encouragement was given to the farmers. This caused shortage of labour in rural Bihar. Famine affected peasants and artisans mainly migrated to cities and after the crisis preferred to return to their original homes.

Famine and death also caused large-scale fall in the cultivated areas. Peasant desertation after the famines of 1770 and 1787 affected agricultural production and artisans.

Thus the famines which occurred during 1770-1800 caused a sharp decline in the economy of Bihar. The extensive rural depopulation and the general dislocation in the economy caused by the famine would have been minor at any period but for the causes discussed above. Their effects were all the worse because these occurred in the context of a labour scarcity which appeared in a chronic form in several districts of Bihar. The recovery was also retarded because of several developments such as the increased revenue pressure on the zamindars, their increasing impoverishment since 1765, and the general stagnation in the economy.

The famines had many dreadful impact on the social life of the people of Bihar as well. As R.C. Dutt remarks "Tender and delicate women whose veils had never been lifted before the public gaze, come forth from those minor chambers in which eastern jealousy had kept watch over their beauty and threw themselves before the passersby, imploring a handful of rice for their children.[29] Slavery, robbery and dacoity were other social effects of the famines in Bihar.

Thus famines in the late 18th century Bihar were the product of natural and man-made factors. The study also shows that the problem of poverty was also one of the main causes of these famines. The administration and some individuals did take steps to manage the problem of famines. But the measures being of a short-term nature could not be a lasting solution to the problem of poverty. One reason was that after the famines were over and people returned to their own homes and lands they did not have enough resources to restart their economic activities. Had there been some governmental support in the form of money or security, the peasants and artisans would have been saved from the hands of the exploitative money-lenders and could have revived their traditional economic pursuits. Moreover the relief measures remained mainly confined to urban areas. The purdah system also proved to be a major handicap in providing relief.

REFERENCES

1. Srivastava, H.S.: *The History of Indian Famines*, Agra, 1971.
2. Ibid.
3. Bihar lies in the geographical heart of India in the Lower and Middle Gangetic region. It has an area of 67,134 sq. miles and is bounded in the north by Nepal, on the west by the states of Uttar Pradesh and Madhya Pradesh, on the south by Orissa and on the east by West Bengal.
4. Lovedy, A.: *History and Economies of Indian Famines*, London, 1914, p. 25.
5. Digby, William: *Prosperous British India*, New Delhi, 1969, p. 123.

6. Marshall, John: *India Notes and Observation in Bengal.*
7. Dutta, R.: *Bengal Past and Present*, Vol. LXXVII, p. 120. The Famine of 1769-70.
8. Diwakar, R.R.: *Bihar Through thc Ages,* p. 610.
9. Bannerjee, D.N.: *Land Revenue System in Bengal and Bihar,* London, 1943, p. 87.
10. Diwakar, R.R.: *op. cit.,* p. 611.
11. Datta, K.K.: *Economic Condition of Bengal Subah 1740-72,* Calcutta, 1936.
12. Bengal Sel. Com. Prog. 1768, pp. 657-58.
13. Hunter, W.W.: *Annals of Rural Bengal,* Reprint–Calcutta, 1965, p. 86.
14. James, J.F.W.: *Selections from the Correspondence of the Revenue Chiefs of Bihar,* Patna.
15. John Shore's Letter to the Committee of Revenue, dated 5 December, 1783.
16. Geddes. J.C.: *Administrative Experience Recorded in Former Famines,* Oxford, 1875, p. 419.
17. Ibid., p. 420.
18. Campbell, George: *Accounts of Famine,* Oxford, 1874, p. 95.
19. Ibid., p. 17.
20. Srivastava, H.S.: *The History of Indian Famines,* Agra 1971, p. 332.
21. Lovedy, A.: *History and Economics of Indian Famines,* London, 1914, p. 68.
22. Letter from the Resident to the Chief of Patna, 1 June, 1770.
23. Select proceedings, Vol. 17, 19 July, 1770, p. 525.
24. Hussain, Ghulam-Siyar-ul-Mutakherin: Translated by Mustafa Haji, Calcutta, 1902, p. 56.
25. Campbell, George: *op. cit.,* p. 127.
26. Farm Committee of Grain to John Shore, 27, October, 1783.
27. Shore, Kalicharan: *Famines in Bengal,* Calcutta, 1844, p. 6.
28. Smith, Adam: *Wealth of Nations,* Vol. II, London, 1917, p. 49.
29. Dutt, R.C.: *Economic History of British India,* Vol. I, London, 1956, p. 52.

7

Governance Disaster: Its Management

AJAY KUMAR JHA

Disaster is a calamity which is suddenly thrust either by nature or by man himself on himself. It blows out, dismantles and smashes all the 'orders of life' haywire. It may occur in any walk of life and at any moment of time. It has a potentiality of putting a man non-plussed. It obviously causes immense loss to mankind. In the twentieth century, if anything has browbeaten mankind so often, it is 'disaster'— disaster of every kind. The more the mankind has progressed and developed, the more it has become vulnerable to the blows of disaster. Disaster keeps on striking in all parts of the world, with almost a 'disciplined regularity'. It may be a sudden outbreak of war at one place. Or, it may be an earthquake at some other place. It may be flood, hurricane, nuclear leakage at some place, or a big fire suddenly flashing and flaming in blocks of apartments at some other place. One may think of any misfortune which suddenly hits human population. And it all has a 'disaster' potential.

But then how to meet the challenges of disaster? It is going to be a towering exercise to the man of the 21st century. To meet the challenges of disaster, we need to evolve some 'universal' and some 'specific' tools which may effectively handle the situation of disaster. Unless we do that, we shall not be able to save the world from great catastrophes to which mankind now seems more vulnerable to, in the years to come. Obviously, disaster management is going to be a vital discipline of study in the next century.

Keeping this proposition in view this study is an attempt to study the dimensions of governance disaster; as the 'governance disaster' in near future, is going to be the most dangerous threat to the largest number of people; spanning from east to west and from north to south of the globe. The style, technique, policies, implementation and execution of such policies have quite often in the past triggered off several incidents of disaster. The governments all over the world have at times initiated such policies which invariably led to a chain of great catastrophes in their respective countries. The nature of such policy implementation in different countries have been quite diverse. From 'apartheid' to 'social justice'—their implementations and executions have sordidly resulted into great social clashes, counter-clashes and even upheavals of great magnitude. Even the developmental policy executions have sometimes resulted in great protests and rebellions by people in several countries. We may, for example, see the questions of policy implementation in the field of environmental pollution, ecological sustenance, etc. However, such cases of policy implementations cannot always be attributed to defective policy formulations at the topmost level. Sometimes even good and socially imperative policies, when implemented or executed, have resulted into disastrous consequences.

Government of India planned a grand project named as Narmada Valley Development Project (NVDP) to the tune of 3 billion pound investment. This project plans for 30 big dams, 135 medium sized ones and 3,000 small dams in Narmada valley. However, the entire project is hanging in balance. The execution of this project is likely to render at least 1,00,000 people homeless. The 40 megawatt Maheshwar dam alone was going to displace at least 2,200 families in 61 villages and destroy thousands of acres of cotton, chillies and wheat (*The Hindustan Times*, 16 January, 1998, Patna, p. 9).

In protest of this project a massive movement has been launched known as Narmada Bachao Andolan (NBA). Only recently in 1997, hundreds of villagers protesting the construction of dams across the Narmada in Madhya Pradesh, took control of the site, forcing the government to suspend the construction work. Sensing the sensitivity of the whole issue, World Bank pulled out of the controversial project five years ago.

Narmada Bachao Andolan protagonists want this project to be completely stopped. They justify their movement on the ground of environment protection as well as humanitarian causes. As a result, a massive developmental exercise of government seems to have been shelved, at least for a while.

Narmada Bachao Andolan which has emerged as a people's protest against the execution of governmental plans is a significant example of governance disaster.

Economic and financial handling of state affairs is one of the most crucial and vulnerable spots where governance can doom disasters for people. There are many governments in the world which have pushed their state to a point of near disasters, if not total disasters. But near disaster situation can very well inaugurate a situation of disasters. Even fifty years of independence of India have not been able to acquire a position of economic power in the world in spite of such huge natural resources and manpower potential, for which it has only itself to blame for. There are many countries in the world which have become economic powers even within forty years of their total destruction.

Only recently in late 1997 and early 1998 the Indian rupee value started falling against dollar to a level where it had never arrived in the past. Governance and quality of governance has lot to offer in this connection, the explanations of economic theories notwithstanding. If the downslide of Indian rupee is not halted at the earliest possible, its balance of payment in relation to other countries may create unprecedented problems for Indian economy. The falling Indian rupee may lead Indian economy to another governance disaster.

However, to understand the gravity of this downslide of Indian rupee, we may examine the mechanism of exchange rate which determines the value of rupee vis-a-vis dollar.

In a floating exchange-rate regime the rates are neither

fixed, nor administered. They are determined by the forces of demand and supply. Demand and supply forces are in turn influenced by a host of ordinary variables, such as inflation rate, rate of interest, balance of current account, etc., and extraordinary variables, such as political upheavals, war, etc. Any change in these variables may lead to changes in the supply and demand schedules and in turn to changes in the exchange rate.

By the mid-1970s, when adjustable peg system was given a good-bye in favour of floating exchange rate regime, various theories were developed explaining changes in exchange rate in the new environment. One such theory was developed by P.R. Allen and P.B. Kenen. The proponents of this approach, known as the balance of payments approach, feel that the differentials in money supply, income growth and in rate of interest between two countries influence the balance of payments and thereby the exchange rate. The first two influence the current account, while the rate of interest influences the capital account through effecting the flow of investment. A favourable balance of payments helps appreciate the domestic currency.

Another school of thought led by J.A. Frenkel is known as monetary approach. Frenkel believes that the three variables as discussed above influence the demand for, and the supply of money and thereby the exchange rate. An increase in money supply causes the domestic currency to depreciate. Similarly, a rise in rate of interest lowers the demand for money which causes further depreciation in domestic currency. On the contrary, a rise in income encourages demand for money and helps appreciate the domestic currency. On the last two counts, the monetary approach thus runs contrary to the balance of payments approach.

The monetary approach was amended by R. Dornbusch who presented a detailed explanation of interest rate impact and who emphasized on the differential inflation rate. In the views of Dornbusch, changes in interest rate influence the exchange rate in two ways. One is that a high interest rate helps enlarge the loanable funds in the money market, as a result of which the domestic currency depreciates. But at the same time, a high interest rate encourages the foreign investment inflow into the country which acts positively on the external value of domestic currency. The Fisher Effect explains further that it is the real interest rate differential that matters.

Again, as far as inflation rate differential is concerned, it is also very important in determining the exchange rate. The explanation is based on the Purchasing Power Theory and the theory of one price. It means that the currency of a country with higher inflation rate loses its purchasing power and hence depreciates vis-a-vis foreign currency. It is because of this the pre-inflation exchange rate cannot be sustained.

Again, there are economists who believe that it is not the supply and demand for money alone that determine the exchange rate. But it is the entire portfolio of financial assets that has an impact on the exchange rate. Mckinnon, the leading proponent of this school of thought argues that growth in budgetary deficits leads to growth in domestic bonds which leads to monetisation of debt and an increase in money supply. Current account surpluses cause an increase in holding of foreign bonds. In both the cases, domestic currency will tend to depreciate. If domestic interest rates go higher, demand for foreign bonds and thereby demand for foreign currency will be lower. Domestic currency will appreciate. Thus changes in the preference for money, domestic and foreign bonds influence the exchange rate.

In a forward market, the size of premium or discount depends mainly on the current expectations of future events. Suppose if dollar is expected to depreciate, the holders of dollar will start selling it forward. The forward sale will help depress the forward rate of dollar. The explanation of forward differential finds an important place in the theory of interest rate parity. This theory states that the currency of a country with lower interest rate should be at a forward premium in relation to the currency of a country with higher interest rate. More precisely, the forward differential should approximately equal the interest rate differential for each maturity.

Rupee is on managed float. Any variation in its value is natural. The RBI can intervene in the foreign exchange market in order to stabilize its value. The recent fall in the value of rupee is nothing new. In October, 1995, there had occurred a drastic fall and so was in February, 1996. This time too, rupee has experienced a substantial depreciation which goes to about 10 per cent. The value of rupee, which was Rs. 36.1 per dollar on October 24, 1997 dropped to Rs. 39.50 per dollar by the 1st of December. Such a scenario involves primarily three questions. One is, what should be the size and frequency of RBI's intervention. The other is, what are the possible causes for the drastic fall. Last is whether the package introduced by the RBI should prove efficacious.

The RBI sells dollar in the foreign exchange market as a result of which supply of dollar increases vis-a-vis rupee. Rupee tends to appreciate. On the other hand, purchase of dollars by the RBI helps rupee to depreciate. This is the intervention by the RBI. But the question is whether intervention should be a routine affair or it should be very rarely used leaving in normal cases the exchange rate to represent the macro-economic fundamentals. Arguments for both the possibilities are there. However, in the Indian case, the RBI feels that it should not be frequent. At the time of the recent fall of rupee, it was said that the fall was long overdue in view of maintaining export performance in the wake of the depreciation of some South-East Asian currencies.

At a seminar on the occasion of IMF-World Bank meeting in Hong Kong in September 1997, it was stated that "competitive devaluation would soon become a policy issue... the question will arise, sooner or later, as to how India will retain competitiveness if South-East Asian currencies have depreciated so sharply." Rangarajan's policy of least intervention is not devoid of realities, especially in view of the fact that the South-East Asian countries are India's main competitor as far as agricultural exports and export of textiles are concerned. Both taken together account for almost one-half of India's total export earnings. If depreciation of rupee is not checked at least to a reasonable extent, Indian exports will fare better.

But such a thinking is not beyond doubts. It is because rupee has depreciated by about 10 per cent vis-a-vis 45 per cent depreciation of Thai Baht; 32 per cent depreciation of Malaysian Ringitt; and 28 per cent depreciation of Indonesian Rupiah. On the contrary, India's import bill will inflate as many imports are price-inelastic. Some of the petro-products like diesel are indexed to international prices and so, a fall in Indian rupee would mean higher prices of petro-products. Costlier imports will not only affect the current account balance but also push the domestic prices. Depreciated rupee will enhance the servicing cost of external borrowings. Budgetary deficit will be hit this way. Rupee depreciation will erode the earnings of the foreign institutional investors from the capital market in India and enhance their exchange risk. This is perhaps the reason that their net investment in Indian capital market dropped from Rs. 345 crores during 2-24 October, 1997 to Rs. (–)199 crores during 24 October, to 4 December, 1997, that is when rupee depreciated.

If RBI goes for aggressive intervention to arrest any depreciation in the value of rupee and if it fails to do it, foreign exchange reserves will be badly hit. In fact, during the recent debacle, this actually happened.

In recent times, a lot of issues with regard to governance have been boiling in the minds of policy-makers. One such issue is the call of "bandhs". Bandhs have in recent times caused a lot of disasters, related with governance. On many important occasions, against certain decisions of the government, call for bandhs have been given by several opposition political parties and other interest groups. These bandh calls have literally paralysed government functioning. As a result any call of bandhs in essential services were declared illegal.

But recently even general calls of 'bandhs' have been declared illegal and unconstitutional in India by a ruling of Supreme Court of India. It has sparked a debate of immense magnitude. How far the bandh calls are responsible for disasters? Are the bandh calls results of governance disasters? Are the bandh calls genuine? Will they really help the cause of people?

Is the illegal declaration of bandhs called by political parties, trade unions and other organizations a 'cruel slap' on people's democratic rights or a crucial step to restore the fundamental rights of individuals? The verdict confirming a Kerala High Court order has already launched a debate.

There is considerable opinion that bandhs, ensuring total closure of all activity in a city or across a state, is a normal way of protest. Some feel the protests could be conveyed through partial closures, although 'mass movements' were acceptable to arouse public awareness. Talk has also started to look for 'alternative' methods of protest.

The 'bandh' was used by veteran Communist leader S.S. Dange in the early sixties to organize protests that had mass participation. The All India Trade Union Congress (AITUC) that he led did a lot of preparatory work to arouse sympathy for its actions. The practice was initially followed by political parties and trade unions so that bandhs were successful and not hated. Down the years, the groundwork was neglected and an element of coercion introduced.

It is widely believed that as a form of protest the bandh had evolved during the freedom struggle itself and the nation's top leaders gave numerous calls to people to suspend all work to convey how serious they were.

Analysing the judgement, Communist Party of India (CPI) general secretary A.B. Bardhan says that the Supreme Court order denies the 'basic right' of the people to voice their grievances and demands through agitational means. The bandh was one of the agitational methods that was devised by the Indian working people in the course of their movement.

Mr Bardhan says, "I may understand if they expect certain regulations to be followed. But a blanket ban, that too confirmed by the Supreme Court, is a serious infringement of democratic rights". Hundreds of bandhs had been organized in the country and one would not say that anything untoward had happened. If it was a question of inconvenience caused, then one could even argue that a procession also caused inconvenience.

"Is it not a fact that the movement of VVIPs also causes inconvenience to the ordinary people? Are we therefore for stopping the movement of VVIPs?" asks Mr Bardhan. He feels the Supreme Court failed to take into account that people had a right to voice their grievances. Freedoms guaranteed under the Constitution could be taken away by the judgement. Its impact could operate against the weaker sections and for the doubtful conveniences of the more affluent.

AITUC deputy general secretary H. Mahadevan says the trade unions were not merely worried about their demands. The issue was not just legal but had social aspects. How could social change be effected without protest, he asks. The bandh was just a form of protest. "Change without protest is not possible. Prayers will not bring about change", he says.

A trade union leader who himself organized bandhs. Mr. Mahadevan says bandhs always exempted essential services like water, milk supplies, fire and medical services. "We are part of the society. We don't want to behave irresponsibly", he says.

The Supreme Court judgement does not go into social situations which could arise suddenly, "Anyway, we are not cowed by the judgement. With rich experience in the field, we will not be found wanting in alternative methods of protest", he says. Solidarity actions were often organized to express support on various issues. A fundamental right to protest, and that too supported by ILO conventions, could not be given up easily.

Striking a different note, Bharatiya Mazdoor Sangh (BMS) leader R.K. Bakhi says his union had at no stage taken part in any Bharat Bandh or a state-level bandh. Even though the union was strongly opposed to the new economic policies, it did not take part in a bandh. "We are for industrial bandhs and not for total bandhs", he says.

The union feels that the new economic policies could increase the American stranglehold over the Indian economy and would organise a "mass movement" in June next year. The union would go to villages and mobilise the people against the policies in the same manner as Mahatma Gandhi used to do.

The judgement has upset the Left movement. Communist Party of India (Marxist) politburo member Prakash Karat says that by upholding the Kerala High Court verdict, the Supreme Court had entered an area which was in the domain of "political activities". The judiciary, he says, should not be "decreeing what is the acceptable form of political or public protest action."

The bandh was not an instrument of protest to be used casually. It was always resorted to when a wider and higher form of protest was required to express popular grievances. The judgement, according to Mr Karat, was predisposed to the viewpoint of the propertied classes and those who were not victims of the present socio-economic system. It sought to enforce a directive which was neither feasible nor advisable in a democratic system.

The very word 'bandh' evokes images of closed shops, patients dying for want of medical care and empty streets with remains of burnt vehicles. Little wonder then that the recent Supreme Court ruling upholding the Kerala High Court judgement declaring that bandhs are a violation of the Fundamental Rights has won plaudits from several senior politicians and legal experts. The distinction made by the apex court between voluntary participation and the use of coercion to make the protest successful has been lauded by the general public.

This form of protest was initiated in India by Mahatma Gandhi against the Rowlatt Act in 1918. The target of his protest was an alien regime. In the present context, a bandh paralyses everyday life and the sufferer is the common man and the loser the nation.

As an instrument of protest against British imperialism, the bandh proved its efficacy. With life, business and industry coming to a standstill, the worst hit was the ruling class. Today, apart from hardship for the daily wagers who constitute a huge chunk of the floating population in the metropolises, it spawns violence and loss of life and property. Equally serious is the damage to industry and the national economy in terms of productivity and the man-days lost.

Bandhs completely jeopardize the functioning of business, industry and normal life. The Supreme Court has heeded the voice of the public and done the right thing. Those calling for a bandh must realise that they as citizens, have to work. They have no right to bring this to a halt.

But as a means for ventilating grievances, bandhs have lost their mass appeal. The participation in such events are generally confined to party cadres. The politics of agitation is, in fact, an anachronism in the urban ambience dominated by the service sector. Not surprisingly, therefore, political parties are hard put these day to even mobilize crowds for public meetings. Consequently, the organizations calling for bandhs end up resorting to violence to make their protest appear successful.

A bandh is a visible form of protest, it is a clear and constant reminder about the issue against which the protest has been organized. As such it is a very effective means of protest, explains civil liberarian, Prashant Bhushan. But with the political parties giving bandh calls for all the wrong reasons, he says. This form of protest has become trivialized.

There is also the tendency for the ruling party to collaborate with the organization calling for a bandh, if it serves its purpose, and opposing it if it does not. Bandh calls on issues lacking mass involvement are destined to fall.

If any decision is against the interests of a political party, a bandh call is given. The decision may not necessarily be against the interest of the people, yet they are sucked into the protest.

Bandhs have thus a lot to contribute to governance disaster. Likewise, governance disasters have a lot to contribute to such bandh calls too.

Governance disasters can also be seen in the way law and order of the state is handled. In developing countries, rising unemployment, spiralling prices, poor quality of life, political immaturity of leadership all combine to create a situation where governance becomes so bad that it often results in disasters. As a result crime rates go alarmingly higher and higher.

In recent times, we can take the case of Andhra Pradesh. Crime rate has sharply increased here which is a testimony of governance disasters.

The banned People's War Group (PWG), the most militant of all the extremist groups operating in the State, began in the year '97 with a major offensive on January 10 blasting the Karakagudem police station in Khammam district killing 16 policemen, the largest number of casualties in an extremist attack against the police. Eighty Naxalites belonging to four *dalams* (armed squads) had surrounded the police station and carried out the attack in the early hours in a meticulously planned operation.

While the extremists killed 165 people, including 47 policemen, the number of murders committed in 1997 stood at 245 including the slaying of 51 policemen (one deputy superintendent of police, one circle inspector, four sub-inspectors and 39 constables). The extremists had carried out landmine attacks against policemen on six occasions.

The number of extremists killed in encounters was 146 in 176 cases of exchange of fire while 132 Naxalites were killed in 135 encounters during the year.

With the PWG setting out a violent agenda aimed converting the Telangana and Dandakaranya regions (comprising parts of Andhra Pradesh, Maharashtra, Madhya Pradesh and Orissa) into guerrilla zones, the attacks on public and private properties as also on political representatives registered a sharp increase. The State Government was forced to renew the ban on PWG and to ask the Centre to deploy additional Central paramilitary forces in the Naxal-dominated regions.

Bidding adieu to its poll promise to implement total prohibition in the State, the ruling Telugu Desam Government relaxed the dry law by permitting the sale, manufacture and consumption of Indian-made Foreign Liquor (IMFL) through an amendment to Andhra Pradesh Prohibition Act, amid protest from opposition members in the Assembly and women's groups outside.

Chief Minister Chandrababu Naidu justified the move on the grounds that it had become difficult to enforce dry law in toto in the State with none of the neighbouring states having prohibition. Besides it was leading to the emergence of gangs of bootleggers and mafias indulging in illicit liquor trade.

Other states are not far behind. Let us take the case of Bihar. Apart from general and sporadic crimes spreading in the length and breadth of Bihar, the organized group crime has taken a very ugly turn. They all demonstrate in themselves different forms of governance disasters.

A chronology of events given in Table 1 is illustrative of this fact.

TABLE 1
CRIMES IN BIHAR DURING 1984–97 SHOWING GOVERNANCE DISASTERS

Year	*Incident*	*Casualty*	*Group Involved*
1984	Danwar-Bihta (Bhojpur)	29	CPI-ML and landlords
1986	Arwal (Patna)	24	Police killed 24 party unity cadres.
1987	Dalelchak-Baghoura (Aurangabad)	54	MCC kills landlords
1991	Tiskhora (Patna)	15	CPI-ML activists killed by Kisan Sangh.
1991	Deo Sahiara (Bhojpur)	15	CPI-ML kills landlords
1992	Bara (Gaya)	34	MCC kills landowners
1996	Bathanitola (Bhojpur)	22	Ranbir Sena kills CPI-ML activists.
1997	Haibaspur (Patna)	10	Ranbir Sena kills Dalits
1997	Jalpura (Patna)	11	PU kills landowners

Governance disasters have not only taken its toll in developing countries like India, it has also taken a very heavy toll in developed countries. They cannot only be seen in the area of economic performance, law and order, crime, insurgency, etc., but also in the area of polity itself take, for example, elections. What is the price, a country like India has to pay if elections occur every now and then on account of governance mismanagement. They spell out great disasters for the people—as it is the people who bear the entire cost of such untimely elections. India has had to hold the third successive election in 1999, in the past three years (13 Lok Sabha) when the BJP government was voted out of power after 13 months of rule.

Estimates suggest that in 1996 general elections for Lok Sabha (11th Lok Sabha) Election Commission itself spent Rs. 500 crores. Compared to this last ten general elections in India put together cost the tax payers about Rs. 607.22 crores. While the first poll cost the country Rs. 10.45 crores, the expenditure on the conduct of elections in 1991 crossed Rs. 300 crores. And by 1996 it touched a whopping Rs. 508.68 crores. In the 1998 elections it is likely to cost the tax payers around Rs. 800 crores.

Apart from these election expenditures let us calculate the price which the country might have paid with frequent change of government at the centre. After 1st December, 1989 when Rajiv Gandhi was voted, out India has till date six prime ministers. Out of these six prime ministers only Narasimha Rao lasted for about five years. Among the rest none could exceed 350 days in office. V.P. Singh lasted for 341 days, Chandra Shekhar lasted for 224 days, H.D. Devegowda lasted for 325 days. I.K. Gujral also did not last for a year. Atal Behari Vajpayee came in as Prime Minister in the 12th Lok Sabha. His government was voted out of power after it had completed 13 months of governance after great difficulty in April 1999.

The cost of these changes are nothing less than disastrous for people of India.

We would therefore, conclude that governance disasters are in fact much more serious issue today than anything else. It must be seen in right perspective to arrive at anything meaningful for the people and the polity.

8

Disaster Management and Coal Industry: An Indian Experience

S. K. CHOWDHARY

Introduction

Of all the peace time professions, the underground coal mining is by far the most hazardous one. This is the universal experience in all the countries where underground coal mining is being carried out. There have been disasters in coal mines in every coal producing country of the world.

In UK during fifty years from 1850 to 1900 there were over 10,000 fatalities in about 2200 explosions. In USA during the period 1911 to 1955 there were over 1,600 deaths in 315 explosions. Table 1 lists some of the disasters owing to explosions in different countries.

TABLE 1
DISASTERS DUE TO EXPLOSION WITH THEIR CASUALTIES

Sl. No.	*Country*	*Mine*	*Year*	*Number of Deaths*
1.	FRG	Luisenthal	1962	299
2.	Japan	Mikawa	1963	457
3.	Japan	Yamana	1965	331
4.	India	Dhori	1965	268
5.	Yugoslavia	Orasi Shaft	1965	144
6.	USA	Farmington	1968	78
7.	Yugoslavia	Breza	1970	51

In India since 1901 (i.e. the year when first Mines Act came into force) over 2,000 persons died in 50 mine disasters as given in Table 2 :

TABLE 2
FREQUENCY OF DISASTERS IN INDIAN COAL MINES

Sl. No.	*Period*	*Number of Disasters*	*Number of Persons Killed*
1	1901-1910	4	57
2	1911-1920	9	149
3	1921-1930	4	114
4	1931-1940	6	349
5	1941-1950	4	52
6	1951-1960	9	391
7	1961-1970	2	282
8	1971-1980	7	518
9	1981-1990	3	45
10	1991-1996	2	111
Total	1901-1996	50	2068

However, it has to be appreciated that India today ranks third amongst coal producing countries of the world with its production reaching nearly 300 million tonnes during the current year 1997-98 and expected level of production during 2006-2007 would be nearly 570 million tonnes. Indian coal industry is labour intensive with an average daily employment of nearly 5,60,000 in 575 mines. Mining being one of the most hazardous peace time occupations, it is but natural that when such a large workforce is employed in mines, the total number of casualties in mine accidents will be comparatively higher. Though the absolute number of fatalities is comparatively higher, yet the rate of fatalities per thousand persons employed is nearly 0.32 which compares favourably with many of the advanced coal producing countries. However, one of the disturbing features of the accident experience is that there have been as many as 50 disasters killing 2068 persons during the current century. In India an accident involving 10 fatalities or more is termed as disaster. These disasters have caused severe damage to the industry, society and economy apart from loss of life.

Some Major Disasters

Disaster in Chasnalla colliery on 27.12.1975 killed 375 persons in a matter of few minutes. The accident was caused due to accidental connection of the workings with waterlogged old workings in a 24 metre thick seam dipping at 1 in. 1.5. The workings contained nearly 500,000 cubic metres of water. A dip drivage nearly 49 metres (inclined distance) had been made in the past from the dip most level of the old workings. The existence of this drivage was reportedly not known. The method of development in the new workings (shaft workings) was to drive level galleries along the foot wall and hang-wall and connect them with cross cuts. One of such cross cuts being drive from hangwall to footwall punctured into the 49 metres old drivage mentioned above. Illustrative sketch at Annexure 2 may be seen. Recovery of dead bodies could be done only after 23 days since the management was not ready for pumping of such large quantities of water.

Disaster in Dhori colliery on 28.5.1965 was another mass killer. 268 persons lost their lives in an explosion. Till the time of accident, the mine was treated as non-gassy mine and naked lights (hurricane lights) were used in the mine for the purpose of illumination. There was no mechanical ventilator, the air being circulated by natural ventilation only. The enquiry into the causes and circumstances leading to the disaster revealed that there was an accumulation of firedamp within explosive limits in a level gallery. It was ignited by the hurricane iantern of a person who entered this gallery. As a result of this ignition, a firedamp explosion was caused and as there was enough fuel in the form of coal dust in all parts of the mine, a coal dust explosion was initiated by the gas explosion which soon spread to all other parts of the mine.

The Court of Enquiry into the causes and circumstances leading to the accident made some important recommendations which are given in Appendix 3. These recommendations were later incorporated in the Coal Mines Regulations.

A very unusual disaster resulted in 10 fatalities at Jagannath opencast mine on 24.6.1981. Fourteen workers present at a distance of about 60 metres from the quarry face were suddenly engulfed in a cloud of hot ash and were severely burnt. Ten of them succumbed to their injuries.

The incident is the only one of its kind in this country and as far as is known, it has no parallel anywhere else also.

There was a fire in one of the quarries. Prior to the accident there was heavy rainfall for four days. Total rainfall during these four days was 162 mm. A pump was being installed on the quarry floor and the foundation job for this pump was awarded to a contractor who had engaged 13 workers for this work. A supervisor, a pump operator and the contractor were present around the place. At about 1 p.m. when some of them were coming out of the quarry for lunch, they heard a noise of rolling stones and saw a stream of stones rolling down from a height of about five metres above the quarry floor. As they started running, they felt that sound of the sliding material was increasing and they noticed a dense cloud of smoke and dust above them. They received serious burn injuries. Ten of them received 80 to 100 per cent burn injuries and succumbed to their injuries. The remaining persons had lesser burn injuries and they survived. After the accident, the quarry bed was found covered with ash and clinker which had spread in a fan shaped area with an arc length of 210 metres and radius of 90 metres. The thickness of ash varied between 0.5 cm and 25 cm.

The Court of Enquiry concluded that under the circumstances prevailing at the time of the incident, there was a possibility of generation of superheated steam at high pressure. The heavy rain on four days prior to the incident could have clogged the cleavage planes and other natural fissures in the coal and associated rocks and steam superheated to about 800° F. could be entrapped at a pressure of 350 p.s.i. or more, in the interstices of ash and strata. The slight movement in the coal face was the forerunner of the outburst and large seal slide of the side occurred only after the ejection of the material from the fire-zone.

The Court of Enquiry recommended inter-alia that the phenomenon of spontaneous heating and the measures to deal with fire in opencast mines need to be investigated thoroughly by a High Power Body which should evolve guidelines for the industry to deal with the problem.

Disaster Management

Requirements of disaster management plan comprise two aspects namely prevention of disaster and action for speedy rescue and recovery, should a disaster strike. Since the disasters in mines occur due to varied causes, the management plans will vary according to the cause.

Each and every explosion and ignition of inflammable gases has the potential of a disaster. Adequate ventilation is the first line of defence against a firedamp explosion. Regulation 130 of the Coal Mines Regulations, 1957 of India lays down the standards of ventilation in mines. The requirements of quantity and velocity of air vary with the degree of gassiness of mines. Indian Coal Mines have been categorized in three degrees of gassiness-degree I being the least gassy and degree III being the gassiest with firedamp emission of 10 m/tonne of coal production or more. The standards laid down are considered adequate. Although the Coal Mines Regulations do not provide for continuous monitoring of inflammable gas, quantity and velocity of air, yet Fifth Tripartite National Conference on Safety in Mines held under the Chairmanship of Union Labour Minister in the year 1980 recommended that all third degree of coal mines should have a comprehensive network of environmental monitoring system including methane monitoring.

In spite of best efforts, the possibility of occurrence of inflammable gas in explosive limits in the workings cannot be ruled out and therefore, safeguards against source of ignition have been provided in Coal Mines Regulation and Indian Electricity Rules. A critical analysis of ignition and explosions during the last 25 years reveals that most of such incidents were caused by electric sparks. There are provisions for use of flameproof enclosures and intrinsically safe electrical circuits in critical locales. What is important is to ensure that such enclosures and circuits are maintained properly to remain safe.

It is a well-known fact that many of the coal dust explosion with serious consequences are caused by methane gas ignitions. Therefore, provisions have been made in the Coal Mines Regulations for reducing formation of coal dust, preventing the dust from getting air-borne, rendering the dust non-inflammable and finally arresting the propagation of an explosion, should one occur. The provisions are considered adequate.

Inundations in Indian coal mines have taken place from surface source and from waterlogged workings below ground. There are provisions in the Regulation for obtaining approval of the Directorate General of Mine Safety (DGMS) while extending workings beneath and with 15 metres of the ponds, rivers and water courses. While granting such approvals, DGMS lays down conditions which vary from mine to mine depending upon the local conditions. However, as a general rule, permission for development beneath rivers, canals and other water courses is given only where the hard cover is atleast 15 metres. Similarly while working near rivers and other water courses, mine openings are required to be atleast 1.5 metres above the highest flood level.

For prevention of inundation from underground sources, permission from DGMS is required while extending working within 60 metres of any waterlogged workings. Many of the disasters due to inundation were caused by inaccurate mine plans. The matter was considered by Fifth Tripartite National Conference on Safety in Mines and the Conference made a recommendation which are given in Annexture 4.

When a disaster occurs in a mine, first few hours are most vital for rescue of men and saving the property. The Coal Mines Regulation provide for emergency plan in case of every underground mine. The plan must specify the action by different persons viz. attendance clerk, Junior Supervisors, Senior Supervisors, etc., so as to avoid confusion. However, in actual practise it has been experienced that due to lack of awareness of the provisions of such plan, much time is lost. Further, unruly action of mob has been found to hamper actual rescue operations. There is, therefore, need for a plan which is well rehearsed at regular intervals. The plan must make provision for adequate help from the state administration who is responsible for maintaining law and order.

Mines Rescue Rules are applicable to all mines employing 100 persons or more below ground. The rules provide for maintaining rescue stations and rescue rooms and employment of adequate field volunteers for facing any emergency. The rules are adequate for the time being. What is required is a strict control on training of rescue personnel and maintenance of adequate rescue equipment so that in the event of emergency, the rescue personnel are not handicapped in any way. Needless to say that rescue organization must have good communication and transport facilities.

It has been experienced in case of several emergencies that rescue operations were hampered since the means of ingress were blocked due to explosion or inundation. Therefore, every mining company should provide an emergency winding arrangement and facilities for drilling large diameter book holes. It may be mentioned that availability of drill rigs enabled rescue of 66 persons trapped in Mahabir colliery due to inundation in the year 1989. These persons were rescued through a large diameter bore hole in a capsule. The hole was drilled from the surface.

To cope with any disasters in future, it would be worth attempting development of the following:

(a) A self-contained breathing apparatus as light as possible and capable of providing oxygen for an hour.

(b) Strategically located portable shelters, capable to withstand secondary explosions and containing life support for a group of men.

(c) Seismic sensing system capable of locating trapped men in a mine or air pockets.

(d) Instruments for remote scanning of 'in-mine' conditions.

(e) Devices to locate and delineate the exact extent of waterlogged workings.

(f) Drill rigs with high penetrating rates capable of drilling holes 15 to 20 cm in diameter for probing trapped miners and drill rigs capable of drilling holes up to 70 cms in diameter and up to 1000 metres depth for rescue of trapped persons.

(g) Radio facilities on site.

(h) Auxiliary generators and portable winding equipment.

(i) Mobile vans (camper type) with bore-hole probing facilities and other equipment.

Conclusion

A mine disaster is the most dreaded event in any mine. There are numerous statutory provisions for prevention of such disasters and dealing with emergencies arising out of such disasters. A sense of complacency, however, prevails since occurrence of such an event in the history of a mine may not be common. Despite good safety record, every mine must prepare for prevention of disaster and meeting any emergency. Every one who has a role to play in emergency. He must be clear about his role so that there is no confusion when any emergency arises. There should be frequent interaction with State Administration for maintaining law and order at the time of emergencies. Trade Union representatives must be taken into confidence so that their help is readily available. There is no provision in our statute regarding providing air tight shelters in underground workings where persons can take shelter if their means of egress is cut off. In highly gassy mines thought may be given for providing such shelters.

Providing good communication from every part of underground workings to the surface and from surface to rescue stations will go a long way in rescue and recovery. A military like discipline is a must for every rescue trained person. A close coordination between Mine Management, Trade Unions and the Government will be a great help in meeting emergencies resulting from mine disasters.

ANNEXURE 1
DISASTERS IN INDIAN COAL MINES

Sl. No.	*Date of Accident*	*Name of the Mine*	*No. of Persons Killed*	*Cause*
1	16.06.1908	Khost	20	Explosion
2	07.02.1910	Disergarh	11	-do-
3	15.10.1910	Sitalpur	12	Roof Fall
4	26.11.1910	Namdang	14	Explosion
5	09.11.1911	Kendwadih	14	-do-
6	11.01.1912	Phularitand	23	Inundation
7	26.06.1913	Jotejanaki	13	-do-
8	22.10.1913	Chowrasi	27	Explosion
9	31.08.1915	Chanda	10	Collapse of pillars
10	04.02.1916	Bhowra	24	-do-
11	20.07.1916	Disergarh	14	Explosion
12	18.11.1918	Disergarh	10	Explosion
13	24.11.1919	Kustore South	14	Rope & Chain breakage
14	28.02.1921	Amlabad	11	Explosion
15	09.03.1922	Khost	13	Explosion
16	04.01.1923	Parbelia	74	-do-
17	14.04.1923	Rawanwara	16	Collapse of pillars
18	17.02.1931	Nimgarh	13	Explosion
19	16.01.1935	Loryabad	11	Inundation
20	19.06.1935	Bagdigi	19	Explosion
21	24.07.1935	Kurhurbaree	62	-do-
22	30.01.1936	Loyabad	35	Fire
23	18.12.1936	Poidih	209	Explosion
24	06.07.1942	Makerwal	14	Inundation
25	22.02.1943	Sodepur 9, 10 & 11 pits	13	Bump
26	08.11.1943	Jamuria 7 & 8 Pits	12	Air-blast
27	19.03.1946	Begunia	13	Explosion
28	12.07.1952	Dhemomain	12	Bump
29	05.08.1953	Majri	11	Inundation
30	14.03.1954	Damra	10	Explosion

(Continued on next page)

(Annexure–1 Contd.)

Sl. No.	*Date of Accident*	*Name of the Mine*	*No. of Persons Killed*	*Cause*
31	10.12.1954	Newton Chikli	63	Inundation
32	05.02.1955	Amlabad	52	Explosion
33	26.09.1956	Burradhemo	28	Inundation
34	19.02.1958	Chimalluri 1 & 2 pits	176	Explosion
35	20.02.1958	Central Bhowra	23	Inundation
36	05.01.1960	Damua	16	Inundation
37	28.05.1965	Dhori	268	Explosion
38	11.04.1968	West Chirimiri	14	Collapse of Stools resulting in Air-blast
39	18.03.1973	Noonidih Jeetpur	48	Explosion
40	09.08.1975	Kessurgarh	11	Roof-fall
41	18.11.1975	Silewara	10	Inundation
42	27.12.1975	Chasnalla	375	Inundation
43	16.09.1976	Central Saunda	10	– do –
44	04.10.1976	Sudamdih Shaft	48	Explosion
45	22.01.1979	Baragoloi	16	Explosion
46	24.06.1981	Jagannath	10	Fire (O.C.)
47	16.07.1982	Topa	16	Roof Fall
48	14.09.1983	Hurriladih	19	Inundation
49	25.01.1994	New Kenda	55	Fire
50	..09.1995	Gaslitand	56	Inundation
		TOTAL	**2068**	

ANNEXURE 2

SKETCH ILLUSTRATING THE ACCIDENT DUE TO INUNDATION AT CHASNALLA COLLIERY ON 27.12.1975 KILLING 375 PERSONS

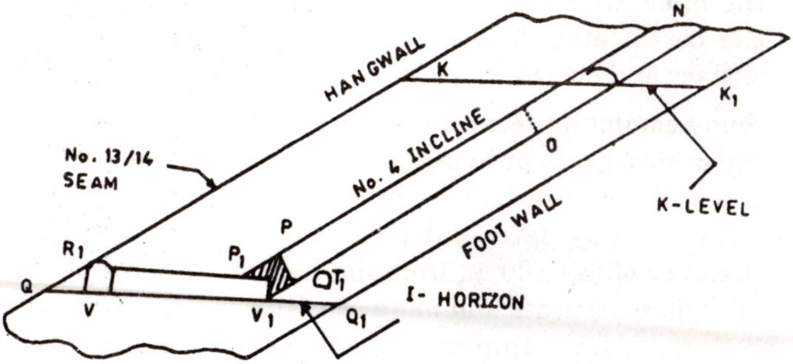

ANNEXURE 3

RECOMMENDATIONS OF THE COURT OF ENQUIRY INTO DISASTER DUE TO EXPLOSION AT DHORI COLLIERY ON 28.05.1965 (268 PERSONS KILLED)

The Court of Enquiry made the following recommendations:

1. Even in non-gassy mines, all workers below-ground should be provided with electric cap lamps.
2. All the mining sirdars, shotfiring sirdars and overmen must be trained to detect the presence of methane in the mine atmosphere. Endorsement for gas-testing on the certificates of all the mining sirdars, shotfiring sirdars and overmen should be revalidated periodically.
3. Some common precautions should be introduced in all the mines, gassy or non-gassy, especially in the working faces. Every mine must be required to test for gas in each working face and also in all places within a distance of say 100 m, from the working face by means of a more accurate and more sensitive instrument than a flame safety lamp or by analysis of samples of air. This should be done by the manager or an under-manager.
4. Even in non-gassy mines, steps should be taken to ensure better ventilation. Regular measurements of air should be taken in all mines.
5. The distance to which a gallery can be driven "blind" must be enforced. Normally, it should be obligatory to make ventilation connections as soon as the gallery is driven a pillar-and-a-half length or 50 m from the last ventilation connection, whichever may be more.

ANNEXURE 4

RECOMMENDATIONS OF THE EIGHTH NATIONAL CONFERENCE ON SAFETY IN MINES FOR PREVENTION OF DANGER OF INUNDATION

1. Mining companies should take immediate steps for training of mine surveyors either by opening specialized courses in the existing institutions or entering into collaborations with Polytechnics or Training Institutes under the Survey of India, etc., for meeting the present and future demand.
2. They should recruit survey apprentices to make good the shortfall in survey personnel. They should take steps to attract and retain qualified and competent surveyors by formulating a suitable Survey Cadre Scheme.
3. Basic requirement for carrying out survey work and for preparing plans in terms of equipment, material and space should be provided.
4. Existing survey personnel should be given refresher training and exposed to modern survey instruments.
5. The work of correlation of mine plans and linking them with the National Grid to the required standards of accuracy should be expedited and completed within a period of one year.
6. For inaccessible, old water logged and other workings, suitable techniques should be developed to delineate them with modern methods of proving.

REFERENCES:

1. Recommendations of the Conferences on Safety in Mines.
2. Reports of Courts of Enquiries into various Mine Disasters.
3. Statistics of Mines issued by DGMS.

9

Industrial Emergency Planning and Disaster Management in Disarray
A Case-Study of Indian Coal Mines

GOVIND P. SHARMA

Introduction

Coal, as the major fossil fuel resource in the country, is of prime importance. It accounts for approx. 85 per cent of the total primary resources of commercial energy and approximately 67 per cent of total energy consumption in India. As per a recent report (1996) of the Geological Survey of India, the country's total coal reserve amounts to 202 billion tonnes which accounts for approximately 6 per cent of the total world coal reserve. There are around about Rs. 592 working coal mines with an investment to the tune of about Rs 160 billion since the nationalization of this sector in 1971-73. The total employees strength of the sector stands at 0.7 million.

After nationalization there is a major shift in coal mining method towards surface mining (opencast) in the last few decades for its being considered more economical (shorter gestational period and higher recovery besides other aspects) as well as safer as compared to the underground mining. Though this has brought new set of challenges and threats in terms of land degradation, water table depletion, erosion, top soil destruction and geological column disruption, social and ecological distortion and large-scale displacement besides a shift in the nature and rate of accidents and casualties with no very significant decline. While in underground mining situation, more accidents occur due to gas emission, water inundation, roof and side wall falls, etc., in opencast situation they are due to heavy machinery, electricity, stumbling, non-planned or ill planned over-burden dumping and improper reclamation.

The industry's safety norms are guided by an exhaustive list of well-structured legislations which are supervised by quite a large internal safety organization of the technocrats and skilled professionals which are further regulated by an external agency. The Directorate General of Mines Safety, so as to ensure their effective implementation and vigilant regulation. The capital input, skilled manpower resources and high technology sophisticated machine deployment are ever increasing year after year. Utmost importance and emphasis are given on the labour welfare and well-being. But despite all these, a practically effective emergency response plan does not exist at the grassroot level and rescue operation and rehabilitation measures are marked by chaos, shock, trauma, disruption, confusion and societal animosity at large.

This chapter makes a modest attempt to study the coal mining operational dynamics in this context and tries to understand the underlying reasons behind such a situation as regard to accident scenario, emergency planning and disaster management. Based on the official reports and data of the secondary sources with personal observation, queries and social science quest, it also puts forward certain suggestions for amelioration which may be found useful for the working managers of this industry, the social planners and decision makers at different levels.

Nature and Extent of Accidents and Casualties

Four different categories of accidents are recorded while only first two of them are reported. They are: (1) fatal accidents causing deaths; (2) serious accidents causing bodily injuries like vital limb fracture, etc.; (3) any other less serious injury causing absence of the affected person from duty for more than 72 hours, and (4) minor injuries causing absence of the affected person from duty for less than 72 hours. Accidents are generally put to disaster category when more than 10 deaths are involved.

Annexure 1 indicates the trend of fatal as well as serious accidents in Indian Coalfields from 1951 to 1997 while decennial average trend in fatal accidents and fatality rate per 1000 persons employed in coal mining operation is given in Annexure 2 trend in death rate per 1000 persons employed, accident frequency rate per lakh manshifts and rate per million tonnes of coal produced during 1988-97, are represented in Annexure 3. Trends of total fatal and serious accidents and death and serious injury rate during the last 10 years in both underground and opencast mining situations are given in Annexure 4.

Accidents are mainly attributed to noxious gas emissions (Carbondioxide oxide, Carbon monoxide, Methane, etc.), water inundation, rope haulage, fire, roof and side wall fall, etc., cracks or other such subsidence problems, blasting, etc., in the underground mining situation. The problems of inadequate illumination, high temperature, humidity, improper ventilation and lack of adequate fresh air, fire hazards, explosion, strata control, inundation, etc., are thus special areas of safety concern in the underground mining operations. Underground mining contributes approximately 80 per cent of the total fatal mining accidents. The greatest cause of underground mine accidents is the problem of subsidence, followed by rope haulage, water inundation, fire and others.

Opencast mining operation, though less accident prone, especially of the fatal nature, nevertheless contributes quite highly to coal mining accidents and casualties. The factors attributed in this case are non-balanced/specified bench condition, dump side and haul roads, improper condition of heavy earthmoving machinery such as dozers, dumpers and other wheel mounted and trackless vehicles, spontaneous combustion fire during the incubation period or due to improper reclamation, blasting, stumbling, slippage and sudden fall of certain objects. Mechanized opencast mining of today is becoming more accident prone due to non-appropriately planned operation, negligence, ill maintenance of heavy machinery, high voltage regulation and upkeep, lack of proper communication and signalling, rampant adhocism, favouritism and corruption. Approximately 54 per cent of the accidents in Indian opencast mining take place due to machinery problems, while the remaining 8 per cent is attributed to fall of grounds, 12 per cent due to stumbling and slippage, etc., and 26 per cent by other (unclassified reasons).

With increase in capital input, technical manpower resources and sophisticated hi-tech machinery deployment, the accident rates have registered a significant decline after nationalization.

Putting Indian coal mining accident scenario in the global perspective, the country is quite badly placed in a comparative trend of death rate per 1000 persons employed in this industry and death rate per million tonnes of coal production in developed countries like Australia, Japan, USA, France and Germany Annexures 5-7.

Historical Perspective

The term coal is believed to have Sanskrit origin 'Kaal', meaning black. In ancient time it was known as burning rock and was believed to possess supernatural power and quality.

Though some coal was getting extracted for the local consumption even earlier, coal mining, in the form of small surface mines, began in 1774. The first underground mining was started in the shaft mines of Raniganj Coalfields (1814) followed by coal mining in the Central Provinces (1862), in Upper Assam Valley (1881), in Rewa estate (1884) and in Sinhgrauli Coalfields (1887). The real impetus, however, came with demand for coal by the steam engines of the river Steamboats, Railways and Calcutta Jute Mills in the subsequent time. It was raised by various small corporate or non-corporate firms, generally through their appointed agents with sufficient capital base. There were hardly any mining laws or governmental control in such operations and there existed even uncertainty with regard to the ownership of mineral rights and royalties, etc. The mining operation was mostly underground and conventional folk methods of detecting water table and roof and side wall condition monitoring was practised by a Mining Sardar (one who heads a band of mine labourers) through a particular type of stick with silver or brass butt. He experienced the condition through the nature of sound produced when the roof or side was hammered with the butt. The presence of toxic gases was known through observing the behaviour of canary birds carried by the Sardar, which was later replaced by Devy Safety Lamps.

With the beginning of Iron & Steel industry in early 20th century demand for better quality cooking coal started which required professionally skilled manpower and high technology machinery to work with. Teaching of mining as a separate discipline started at Banaras Hindu University (Varanasi), Shivpur (Calcutta) and Indian School of Mines (Dhanbad) during the same period. Various new installations related to ventilation, pumping, environment monitoring devices and electronically controlled alarm system with respective transducers and sensors at different levels, borehole technique of assessing water level and so on came up and went on getting sophisticated day-by-day in terms of their state-of-the-art. This also necessitated the government controls and regulations in coal mining operation.

The first Mines Act was enacted in 1901. This after various revisions gave way to the Indian Mines Act 1952 which currently applies to the mining of all minerals in the country, except the State of Sikkim, including the off-shore mining within the territorial water limits. The first mining rescue station was installed at Kolar Goldfields in 1923, followed by the enactment of the Coal Miners Rescue Rules 1939 as a consequence of series of explosions and fires that happened in coal mines in 1935-36 resulting in heavy loss of lives. The establishment of Mines Rescue Station at Sitarampur and Dhansar followed in 1941, being funded by cess levied on coal production from these regions. Coal Mine Rescue Rules 1939 was replaced by Mines Rescue Rules 1959 and later by Mines Rescue Rules 1985 which is currently applicable. Other two major legislative instruments for safe and smooth coal mining operation viz. the Mines Rule and the Coal Mines Regulations came in 1955 and 1957 respectively. Other allied legislations applicable in coal mining are Land Acquisition (Mines) Act, 1885, Factory Act 1948, Indian Electricity Act 1966, Coal Mines Conservation and Development Act, 1974 and Environmental Protection Act, 1986, etc.

A Bureau of Mines Inspection was set up in 1902 for administering the Indian Mine Act, 1901 with its headquarters at Calcutta. It was converted to the Department of Mines in 1904 with shifting of its headquarters to Dhanbad in 1908. The same organization was renamed as Office of the Chief Inspector of Mines in 1960 and further to its current form as Directorate-General of Mines Safety in 1967.

During the World War I (1914-18), the sudden spurt in demand for coal export, led to excessively ruthless mining, ignoring all safety norms and conservation. The coal mining continued whether soil subsided or some of the mines went into fire. This was followed by the worldwide great economic depression during 1929-33. To maintain the level of profit in depression time, the managing agents of the coal mines went for haphazard easy mining, thus marking the worst period of negligence in both natural and social environment in the Indian coal mining history. To offset the fall in price, the producers increased the production, which led to further fall in the price.

After recovery from the depression time the Second World War (1939-44) generated some demand of coal but the industry could take little advantage due to various constraints like labour scarcity, lack of required mechanization level in mines and so on. Though the rapid growth of iron and steel industry, by this time, gave adequate impetus for modern deep shaft coal mines and a few manually or quasi-mechanized opencast mines to grow, to meet production of the high quality cooking coal. The state did not change substantially in the post-independence time till the nationalization of this industry in 1971-73. The process of transfer of mining rights from the British managing agencies to the Indian businessmen was rather slow and the beneficiaries were generally those associated with the managing agents earlier in coal transportation or other such allied activities. National Coal Development Company was formed in 1956 to regulate coal supply to the railways through corporate structure mining operation, bringing certain changes in the working condition and workers' welfare. Though the major changes in this respect came only after nationalization after the formation of Coal India Ltd (besides a few captive mines of TISCO & IISCO). and its different subsidiary companies. Massive mechanization of both existing underground and manually operated open-cast mines were taken up, besides opening up of the new highly mechanized opencast mines in the newly detected coal bearing regions and emergence of various washeries for coal benefication. Labour welfare, safety and systematic mining through well drawn mine plans were given the utmost importance. Real impetus on development of emergency planning, disaster management, regular rehearsals of the rescue and evacuation was however given only on the recommendation of the Court of Enquiry (1976) on the Sudamdih water inundation massacre.

Safety Organization

Each subsidiary company of the Coal India Ltd. has an internal safety organization to regulate and supervise the fixed statutory safety norms and regulations under guidance of the Directorate-General of Mines Safety (DGMS) which is to inspect each working mine, investigate accidents, emergency responses and planning, grant of statutory permissions, exemptions or relaxation, if any, preview mining projects and working plans, approve all safety equipments, appliances and materials, disseminate safety information and promote safety awareness, conduct periodical examinations and award competency certificates; issue of safety certificates for each working mine operation and works at large as a watch dog for all the safety legislation and statutory norms being strictly followed.

At each working mine, there exists a safety committee with representatives of all disciplines involved in production, pit supervisor and worker's representative which meet every month to oversee all safety issues. At the company's headquarters level, there is a bipartite committee (with representatives from company's side and that from DGMS) and a tripartite committee at the area level (with the representatives from the company's management, DGMS and the workers). A Safety Officer is also appointed in each working mine besides Workmen Inspector from each discipline having rights to inspect the mine.

Each company has one or multiple Mine Rescue Station equipped with all necessary implements and skills to combat any emergency and disaster situation.

Besides taking care of the safety norms to be followed, this organization is also responsible for the occupational health and hygiene of the mine workers.

Emergency Planning and Disaster Management

Mining, being one of the most hazardous industries, poses a formidable challenge in dealing with emergency. More higher and meticulous level of planning, control, checks and balances are required in the entire operation of coal mining along with a thorough risk analysis at each level so as to ensure prevention of any accident or casualty. This becomes more important and necessary in case of old mines where very haphazard mining has been done in the past or otherwise found accident-prone. This is required to be followed by a quite well laid preparedness coupled with alertness, to face the emergency situation in the event of one occurring by any chance. An effective and efficient rescue, recovery, relief and rehabilitation could only then be achieved.

Indian coal mining scenario (barring a few mines of Coal India Ltd. and quite a few privately owned captive ones) is however, quite away from the above, rather an idealistic condition, as it is perceived here by the forward moving capable production managers. Planning process in this industry at various levels of working, by and large, lacks the important component of meticulousness. And even if the same is achieved at the higher or middle level of management, the grassroot situation is not conducive enough to adopt it truly. Adhocism, piecemeal planning, non-integration of different disciplines and components of efforts at various levels of management and working, lack of feeling of belongingness, compartmentalisation and absence of synchronization prevail, thus resulting in the preventive aspect as being mentioned above being largely ignored. Under such circumstances, despite adherence to all statutory norms and regulations the net result in regard to realistic prevention is hardly achieved. The obvious impacts of this scenario are therefore evident in the preparedness too and consequently in the rescue, recovery, relief and rehabilitation operation.

Accidents, minor, serious or major, generally create a chaotic situation of the same progressive degree in Indian coal mines. While it does not remain confined to only a small group of individuals concerned, in case of a minor accident, it becomes a common and only point of concern, not only for the entire workforce at the work site but for their relatives, friends, village fellows, trade union leaders, local petty politicians, pressmen and so on, all of whom gather at the accident site with non-operative attitude and sense of apathy towards the management, in case of major one.

This becomes a great hindrance for the rescue team at work and many a time leads to severe problem of law and order, to be tackled separately alongside the rescue and relief work. At several occasions, the local law enforcing agency and police also do not keep their cool and act with the maturity required at such an extraordinary delicate situation. There is a state of commotion and everything becomes topsy turvy. This severely affects timely rescue, recovery and relief operation. Lack of preparedness and a hand ready working emergency plan aggravate the malaise furthermore. There is psychological breakdown of the remaining unaffected workforce besides loss of production for inordinately longer period. The functioning in the emergency control room is to face lot of interferences and interruptions. The management generally keeps on giving false hopes to the victims' families and relatives which after non-realization create more frustration and animosity. The wild bull chase of the management, the rescue team, the union representatives and the victims' friends and relatives continues. Many times the desired rescue implements are not found in working order and sometimes the readily available rescue brigade does not perform satisfactorily. The exact list of the victims, especially in the underground mining situation, is not readily found due to discrepancies in the attendance register and many times due to absence of the supervising manager from the accident site. This further adds to the problem.

The rehabilitation measures and compensation settlement is another area which is incidentally a state subject being dealt in by the Compensation Commissioner of the respective state, as per the existing Compensation Act applicable at the time of the accident and casualty. The compensation is based on the level of injury and grade of the victim. This too is time taking process with no uniformity and thus adding to the sufferings of the victims' survivors.

Analysis and Suggestions

Coal mining in India is having such a socio-politico-economic background, which gave rise to a typical interest group of the contractors, petty politicians, local trade union leaders and Mafia, having close connivance with the managing agencies. The capital always came from the outside and the earnings from the industry never got linked with the local economy, thus forming an 'enclave'. A particular coal project suddenly brings larger factors of rapid change, amazing the local populace and disrupting the entire socio-ecological equilibrium at large. Rampant corruption prevails at all levels and progressive production enhancement from a particular mining project has remained the prime motive of the managing agencies right from the inception of this industry to the current times. This trend was so in all cases-whether it was managed by a British managing agency in the pre-independence era, or by the Indian non-corporate business class emerged and entrenched out of this industry only or by the public sector undertaking. The labourers have also been largely imported from other parts of the country and the industry remains in the hands of a small 'interest group' whose motive has always been profit oriented. The industry emphasizes to raise production to achieve the ever increasing national target to meet the growing demand of coal and the interest group wishes it further more so, as to enhance their earnings. This emphasis is so much that it leaves little scope for a serious thought on safety and environmental protection, in absence of an inherent focused orientation towards the same. As such, systematic mining with due consideration to the desired level of planning, safety and environmental protection, has never been a part of coal mining working ethos. The illegal mining and trade continues, machinery deployed in mining operation do not get adequate preventive maintenance and the quality of maintenance, whatever and whenever being done, is poor, more as a consequence of the interest group, at work. Many times, thus a disaster is welcomed by this group, as it gives a wider, larger and cleaner opportunity of making exorbitant profits against crash procurement of implements, goods, materials and services to combat the incidence. Though the things have slightly changed after nationalization, the working ethos remaining largely the same, no significant change could be achieved.

The data related to coal mining accidents when put for statistical analysis through a fitted linear regression model (Y=199.419–2.276*X, where X denotes time in terms of year and Y denotes number of accidents) indicates highly significant decline in the incidences of fatal accidents after nationalization of the coal mining industry (i.e. during 1971-97 with F Ratio= 27.859 & R Square = 0.527). However, there is a negative variation in this trend in the last 10 years (1986-97 where Y= 170.303–2.636* X with F Ratio at 9.671 & R Square at 0.492). The same for the serious category of accidents shows quite highly significant decline trend after nationalisation; Y=2011.761–56.864* X with F Ratio at 55.656 and R Square at 0.690. But this has also been slightly affected during 1986-97 (Y=839.379–12.777*X with F Ratio at 0.406 and R Square at 0.039).

The incident of fatal accidents in opencast mining in last 10 years (1986-97) does not indicate a significant decline (Y=25.955 + 0.199 * X with F Ratio = 0.275 and R Square = 0.027). Serious accidents however, have significant level of decline in opencast during the same period (Y=40.530 + 2.329 * X with F Ratio at 6.445 and R Square at 0.392). Both fatal as well as serious accidents have shown highly significant decline during this period (1986-97–Y=144.346–2.836* X with F Ratio at 14.01 and R Square 0.583 and Y = 1006.121–37.762*

X with F Ratio at 25.519 and R Square at 0.747 respectively) in underground mining.

Both death rate as well as serious injury rate per million tonne of coal production have declined quite significantly both in pre-nationalization (1951-71) and post-nationalization (1971-95) period–Y=9.414–0.356* X with F Ratio at 52.023 and R Square at 0.732 for death rate in 1951-71 & Y=3.387–0.128 with F Ratio at 25.970 and R Square at 0.530 for the same in 1971-95 and Y = 86.239–3.195* X with F Ratio at 66.136 and R Square at 0.779 for serious injury rate in 1951-71 and Y=24.305–0.993* X with F Ratio at 154.91 and R Square at 0.870 for the same in 1971-95.

A comparative analysis of the death rate per one lakh persons employed in coal mining in India, France, Australia, Japan, USA and Germany during 1986-96 shows significant variation at 5 per cent (Annexure 7). India, Japan and USA may be grouped in the higher death rate per lakh persons whereas Japan, USA, Germany, Australia and France fall in relatively lower death rate per lakh persons. It is interesting to observe that Japan and USA fall under both groups.

Suggestive Measures

The features and characteristics of coal mining accidents, both in underground as well as opencast operations (more in case of the latter) being largely similar a wide range understanding towards the cause and effects may easily be developed. A comprehensive case history of each mine with an appropriate working contingency/emergency and disaster plan based on the risk analyses of each activity and operation scheduled could be made hand ready along with the mine plan at the worksite. A comprehensive list of experts in different disciplines whose advisory services in a particular nature of emergency could be sought may be appended with the case history and emergency plan.

It is generally found that once the impact of a particular disaster is over, the work is resumed and the disaster is forgotten. It is very essential that each accident, small or big, be thoroughly analysed so as to find out the procedural mistakes for taking up their rectification as follow-up actions.

The pit level safety committee should meet more frequently than at the current interval of one month with more focused orientation and seriousness, followed by a system of immediate compliance against the issues raised in these meetings. More power and authority should be given to a pit/mine supervisor who actually leads the miners' team in the production process to the extent that he may refuse to take up the job the day or shift he finds the working environment not conducive enough from all safety and environmental precautionary angles. It is like a pilot in airlines not ready to take off in case of slightest deviation from the standard norms. The mining safety rules also are required to be reviewed and amended more frequently as per the current need so as to make them more pragmatic. The lag response time in case of any emergency for the rescue team to reach is of prime importance along with its preparedness. It is in this light required that the existing rescue stations be thoroughly revamped and upgraded with more effective and alert rescue brigade.

The evaluation and reward process of the production managers should not only be based on the million tonnes of coal raised, but safety and environmental protection taken up by him for achieving production should also have bearing on the same. Only then the focused orientation towards prevention could be achieved. A manager's performance thus should be judged only on the basis of production figure coupled with the way this figure is achieved and on proper evaluation of his walked out zone. Safety and environmental audits therefore should be made mandatory. It is generally observed that the alertness level among the coal mining workforce is very low, a situation quite misfit in the growing high level mechanization. This is an area of grave concern and appropriate steps are required to be taken up after a proper alertness analysis study based on socio-psychological tools and methodology and appropriate steps be taken up to alleviate the problem through proper inputs of training and motivation.

Further, though there has been much improvement in the material life condition of the mineworkers in recent times, little attempts have been made to raise their educational levels so as to improve the standard of their life condition. Many times the accidents are reported to have occurred due to workers at site being not vigilant due to over exhaustion of working six days a week, sometimes even seven days a week. It is therefore necessary that the working conditions be improved with logical reduction in their working hours.

The preventive occupational healthcare of the mineworkes is another area, which requires adequate attention. The cases of Pneumoconiosis, TB, Silicosis, Asthma and other respiratory disorders, throat and skin diseases, eye irritations, etc., due to dust hazards; Methhaemoglobin, Carbohaemoglobin. etc., due to gas hazards; minor Nystagmus due to illumination problem; Noise Induced Hearing Losses due to noise pollution; Anoxia, TB, Bronchitis, etc., due to ventillation problem, Diarrhoea and other diseases due to water pollution; Weil and other Liver diseases due to humidity and alcoholism besides various psychosomatic diseases like hyper tension, etc., are on the rise. The periodicity of preventive periodic medical examination should be reduced from once in five years currently, to the yearly basis. General noise level and dust hazards have increased with the mechanization of opencast mining, which requires close attention and prevention. The compensation settlement process is also required to be thoroughly studied and some sort of uniformity is to be brought as regard to its level in different provinces.

The entire canvas of problems related to coal mining emergency planning and disaster management has to be seen in the socio-politico-economic background of this industry in India. An effective methodology of bottoms up information flow and tops-down planning process based on an effective and efficient Management Information System and Decision Support System with provision of data capturing at source is of prime importance. All these, however, will work only with a transformation in the working ethos in the coal mining industry that exists today.

TABLE I

TREND IN COAL PRODUCTION METHOD (PERCENTAGE)

	1951	1983-84	1996-97
Open Cast (O/C)	19.43	46.00	71.00
Underground (U/G)	80.57	54.00	29.00

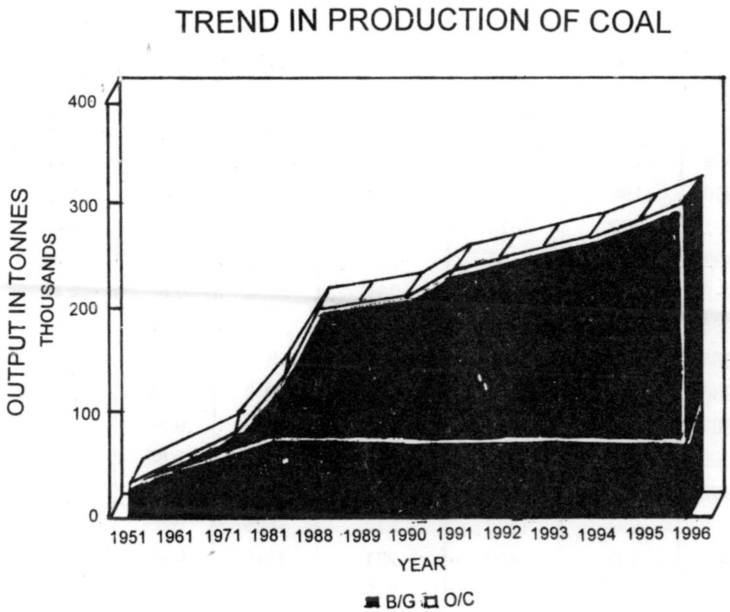

FIGURE I

ANNEXURE 1

FATAL AND SERIOUS ACCIDENTS IN COAL MINES (1951-97)

Year	No. of Fatal Accidents	No. of Serious Accidents	No. of Persons Killed	No. of Persons Injured	Death Rate Per 1000 Persons	Serious Accidents Rate/1000 Persons
1951	278	1893	319	1931	0.91	5.69
1952	293	2529	353	2613	1.00	7.4
1953	257	2741	330	2842	0.97	8.33
1954	221	2760	329	2862	0.96	8.36
1955	215	2780	209	2880	0.89	8.28
1956	199	2762	259	2800	0.73	8.07
1957	165	2678	182	2762	0.49	7.46
1958	208	2797	420	2801	1.10	6.05
1959	191	3052	212	3125	0.55	5.14
1960	198	3258	233	3343	0.59	8.41
1961	222	3515	268	3569	0.65	8.77
1962	229	3125	266	2166	0.61	7.41
1963	223	2443	267	2494	0.59	5.62
1964	163	2005	182	2037	0.42	4.83
1965	175	1939	469	1976	1.10	4.73
1966	196	1934	222	2008	0.55	4.71
1967	195	1865	220	1940	0.59	4.68
1968	212	1765	256	1846	0.65	4.66
1969	211	1650	232	1717	0.61	4.33
1970	294	1577	212	1625	0.59	4.14
1971	199	1460	231	1542	0.42	4.03
1972	200	1534	217	1616	0.53	3.94
1973	172	1904	237	1975	0.50	4.15
1974	200	2066	232	2163	0.46	4.28
1975	222	2135	664	2211	1.26	4.23
1976	209	1800	296	1877	0.58	3.68
1977	216	2093	237	2177	0.47	4.37
1978	163	1902	186	1963	0.37	3.94
1979	148	2051	184	2122	0.37	4.24

(Continued on next page)

ANNEXURE 1 *Contd.*

Year	*No. of Fatal Accidents*	*No. of Serious Accidents*	*No. of Persons Killed*	*No. of Persons Injured*	*Death Rate Per 1000 Persons*	*Serious Accidents Rate/1000 Persons*
1980	141	1144	160	1205	0.32	2.41
1981	165	1151	184	1213	0.36	2.36
1982	158	1135	185	1184	0.35	2.23
1983	156	1169	191	1219	0.36	2.28
1984	160	1196	176	1236	0.32	2.24
1985	176	1007	204	1060	0.36	1.92
1986	180	1167	214	1199	0.39	2.2
1987	162	190	176	946	0.32	1.72
1988	159	771	175	815	0.32	1.51
1989	156	899	177	946	0.32	1.73
1990	151	893	166	983	0.30	1.79
1991	138	803	143	854	0.26	1.54
1992	165	810	183	894	0.33	1.62
1993	156	854	176	903	0.32	1.65
1994	156	717	241	775	0.44	1.47
1995	137	757	219	813	0.46	1.56
1996	131	677	146	723		
1997*	147	537	169	588		

* Provisional Figures

ANNEXURE 2

TREND IN FATAL ACCIDENTS AND FATALITY RATES PER 1000 PERSONS EMPLOYED (DECENNIAL)

Decennial Year Block	*Avg. No. of Accidents*	*Accident Rate*	*Avg. No. of Fatality*	*Fatality Rate*
1901-10	74	0.76	92	0.93
1911-20	139	0.94	176	1.29
1921-30	174	0.99	219	1.24
1931-40	172	0.98	228	1.33
1941-50	226	0.87	273	1.01
1951-60	223	0.61	295	0.82
1961-70	202	0.49	259	0.62
1971-80	187	0.40	264	0.55
1981-90	162	0.30	185	0.34
1991-97	147	0.28	182	0.35

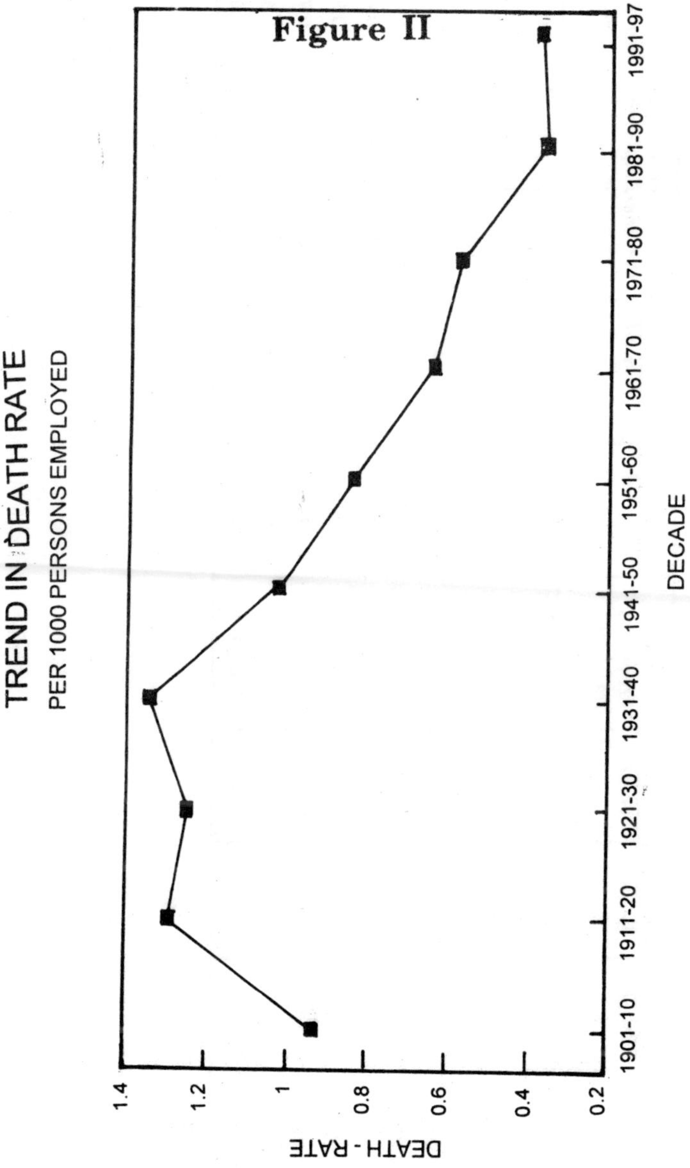
Figure II
TREND IN DEATH RATE
PER 1000 PERSONS EMPLOYED
DEATH - RATE
1.4
1.2
1
0.8
0.6
0.4
0.2
1901-10
1911-20
1921-30
1931-40
1941-50
1951-60
1961-70
1971-80
1981-90
1991-97
DECADE

FIGURE II

ANNEXURE 3
TREND IN FATAL AND SERIOUS ACCIDENTS IN COAL MINES

Year	Number of Accident			Accident Frequency Rate/lakh Manshifts	Number of Persons		Rate per 1000 Persons Employed		Death rate per Million Tonnes
	Fatal	*Serious*	*Total*		*Killed*	*S/injured*			
1988	159	771	930	0.56	175	815	0.32	1.51	0.88
1989	156	899	1055	0.63	177	946	0.32	1.73	0.86
1990	151	893	1044	0.62	166	983	0.30	1.79	0.78
1991	138	803	941	0.56	143	854	0.26	1.54	0.60
1992	165	810	975	0.57	183	894	0.33	1.62	0.73
1993	156	854	1010	0.59	176	903	0.32	1.65	0.68
1994	156	717	873	0.53	241	775	0.46	1.48	0.90
1995	137	757	894	0.57	219	813	0.43	1.58	0.77
1996	131	677	808	0.51	146	723	0.29	1.43	0.48
1997*	147	538	685	0.43	169	588	0.33	1.16	0.56

* Provisional Figures

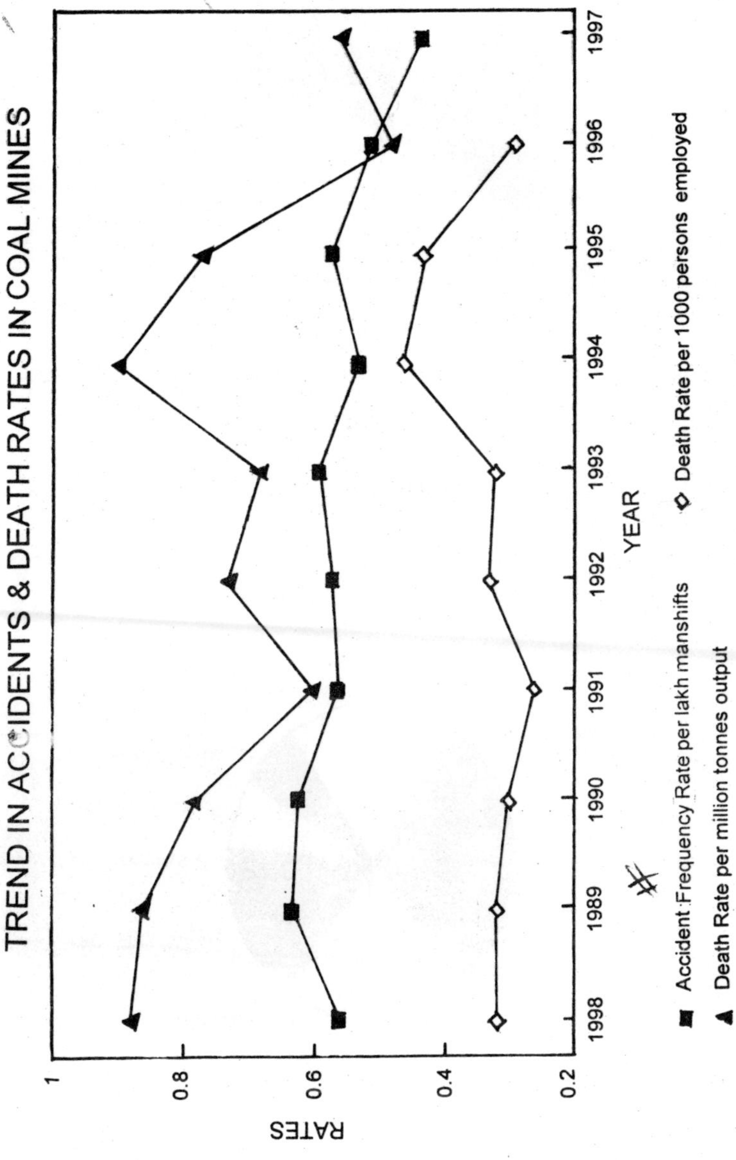
TREND IN ACCIDENTS & DEATH RATES IN COAL MINES
RATES
1
0.8
0.6
0.4
0.2
1998
1989
1990
1991
1992
1993
1994
1995
1996
1997
YEAR
Accident Frequency Rate per lakh manshifts
Death Rate per 1000 persons employed
Death Rate per million tonnes output

FIGURE III

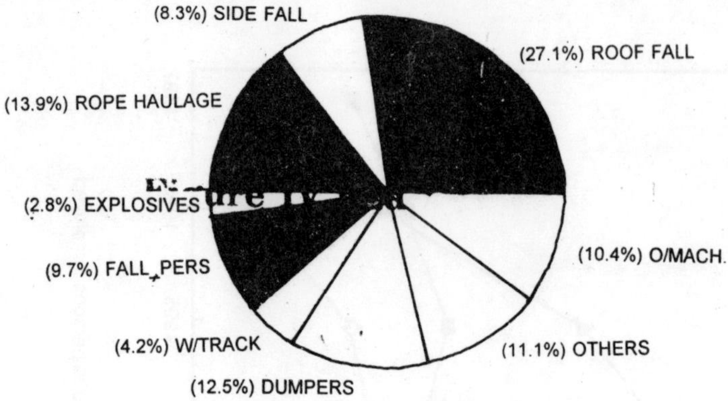

CAUSE-WISE DISTRIBUTION OF FATAL ACCIDENTS IN COAL MINES DURING 1997.

FIGURE IV

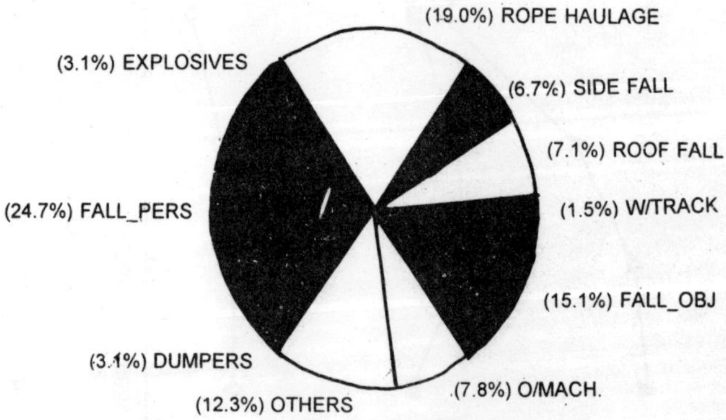

CAUSE-WISE DISTRIBUTION OF SERIOUS ACCIDENTS IN COAL MINES DURING 1997.

FIGURE V

CASUALITIES DURING 1997 BY MAJOR MINERALS

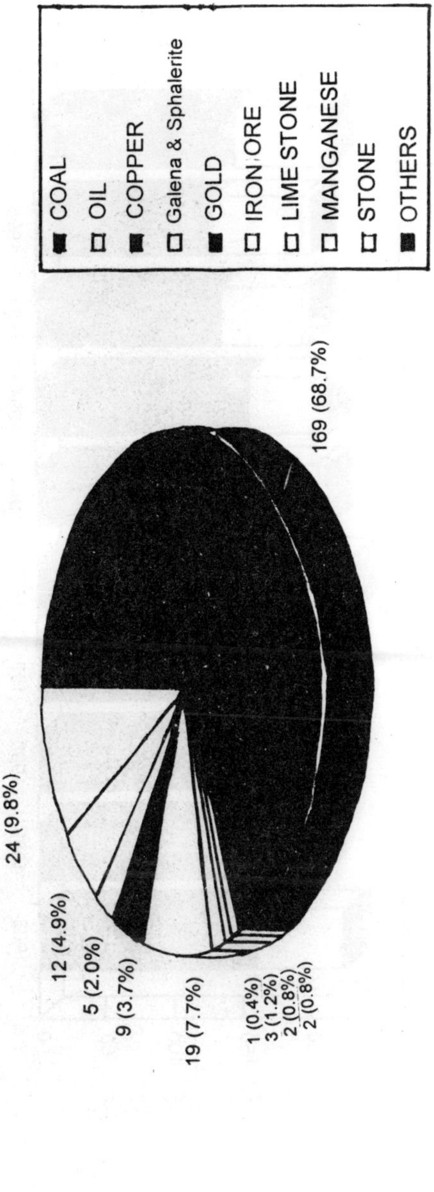

FIGURE VI

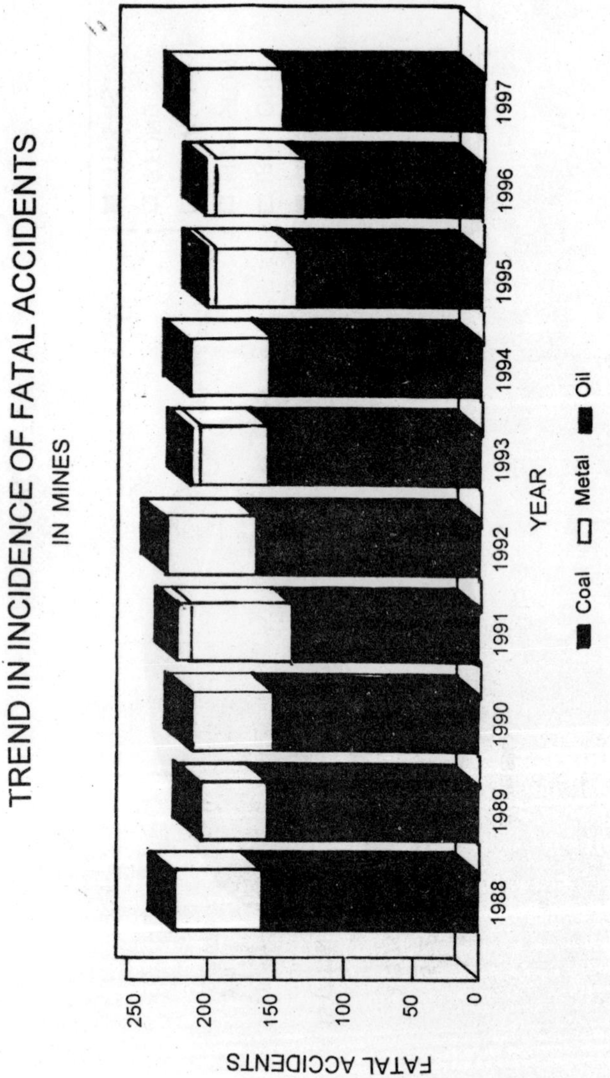
TREND IN INCIDENCE OF FATAL ACCIDENTS
IN MINES
FATAL ACCIDENTS
250
200
150
100
50
0
1988
1989
1990
1991
1992
1993
1994
1995
1996
1997
YEAR
Coal
Metal
Oil

FIGURE VII

ANNEXURE 4

TREND IN FATAL AND SERIOUS ACCIDENTS DEATH AND DEVIOUS INJURY RATE IN COAL MINES—PLACEWISE

Year	Number of Fatal Accidents				Number of Serious Accidents				Death Rate/1000 employed				Serious Injury Rate/1000 Employed			
	Under Ground	Open Cast	Above Ground	Overall	Under Ground	Open Cast	Above Ground	Overall	Under Ground	Open Cast	Above Ground	Overall	Under Ground	Open Cast	Above Ground	Overall
1986	113	27	40	180	935	51	181	1167	0.46	0.45	0.24	0.39	3.08	0.81	1.08	2.20
1987	110	27	25	162	695	33	182	910	0.39	0.44	0.15	0.32	2.29	0.59	1.08	1.72
1988	100	27	32	159	585	31	155	771	0.36	0.45	0.2	0.32	1.97	0.58	0.99	1.51
1989	110	22	24	156	666	62	171	899	0.39	0.42	0.17	0.32	2.21	1.11	1.04	1.73
1990	91	26	34	151	666	69	158	893	0.33	0.42	0.20	0.30	2.38	1.16	0.96	1.79
1991	81	25	32	138	577	60	166	803	0.27	0.39	0.19	0.26	1.96	1.02	0.98	1.54
1992	107	32	26	165	587	49	174	810	0.39	0.52	0.16	0.33	2.14	0.79	1.01	1.62
1993	101	24	31	156	632	57	165	854	0.39	0.37	0.19	0.32	2.19	0.83	1.01	1.65
1994	93	39	24	156	560	50	107	717	0.59	0.64	0.15	0.46	2.08	0.86	0.67	1.48
1995	91	26	20	137	549	69	139	757	0.60	0.38	0.13	0.43	2.07	1.05	0.93	1.58
1996	75	27	29	131	478	71	128	677	0.31	0.42	0.19	0.29	1.83	1.10	0.86	1.43
1997*	94	25	28	147	346	66	126	538	0.41	0.39	0.18	0.33	1.38	1.01	0.84	1.16

* Figures of 1997 are Provisional

ANNEXURE 5

TREND IN DEATH RATES PER THOUSAND PERSONS EMPLOYED IN COAL MINES IN SOME OF THE COUNTRIES

Year	*Australia*	*France*	*India*	*Japan*	*U.S.A.*	*Germany*
1986	0.40	0.12	0.39	0.59	0.47	0.26
1987	0.10	0.11	0.32	0.42	0.37	0.20
1988	0.18	0.30	0.32	0.41	0.31	0.17
1989	0.18	0.19	0.32	0.58	0.43	0.21
1990	0.23	0.09	0.30	0.22	0.41	0.13
1991	0.55	0.20	0.26	0.12	0.38	0.17
1992	0.25	0.17	0.33	0.39	0.35	0.24
1993	0.21	0.00	0.32	0.29	0.33	0.12
1994	0.14	0.13	0.46	0.17	0.31	0.15
1995	0.15	0.14	0.43	0.41	0.36	0.15
1996	N.A.	N.A.	0.29	N.A.	0.31	0.14

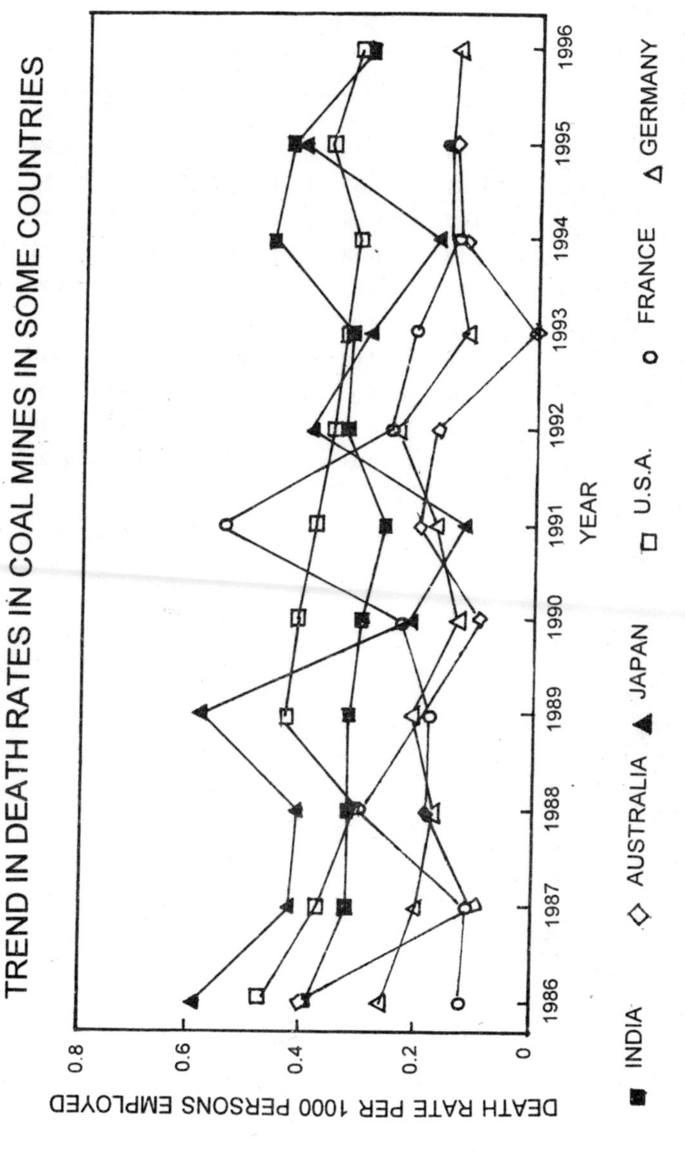

TREND IN DEATH RATES IN COAL MINES IN SOME COUNTRIES
DEATH RATE PER 1000 PERSONS EMPLOYED
0
0.2
0.4
0.6
0.8
1986
1987
1988
1989
1990
1991
1992
1993
1994
1995
1996
YEAR
INDIA
AUSTRALIA
JAPAN
U.S.A.
FRANCE
GERMANY

FIGURE VIII

ANNEXURE 6

TREND IN DEATH RATES PER MILLION TONNES OF COAL RAISED

Year	*Australia*	*France*	*India*	*Japan*	*U.S.A.*	*Germany*
1986	0.10	0.3	1.25	0.93	0.12	0.48
1987	0.02	0.25	0.93	0.61	0.08	0.39
1988	0.04	0.65	0.88	0.53	0.06	0.34
1989	0.03	0.37	0.86	0.68	0.07	0.41
1990	0.04	0.16	0.78	0.24	0.06	0.26
1991	0.09	0.33	0.6	0.12	0.06	0.32
1992	0.04	0.27	0.73	0.39	0.05	0.45
1993	0.03	0.00	0.68	0.28	0.05	0.22
1994	0.02	0.22	0.9	0.14	0.04	0.29
1995	0.02	0.24	0.77	0.32	0.05	0.26
1996	N.A.	N.A.	0.48	N.A.	0.04	0.25

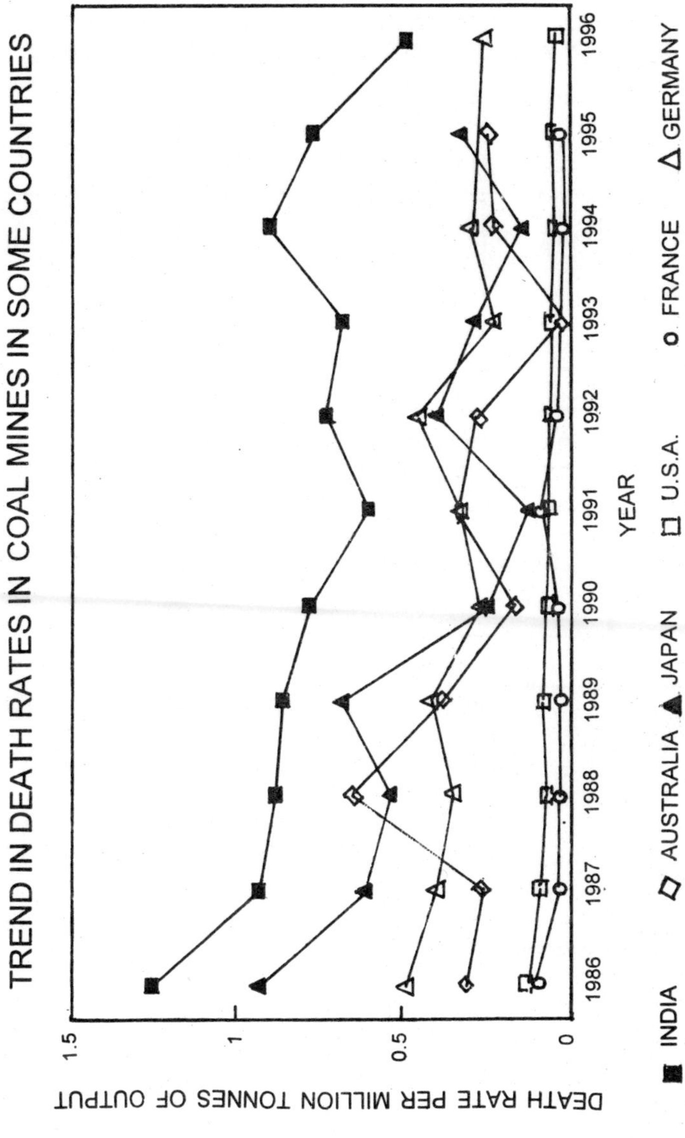
TREND IN DEATH RATES IN COAL MINES IN SOME COUNTRIES
DEATH RATE PER MILLION TONNES OF OUTPUT
1.5
1
0.5
0
1986
1987
1988
1989
1990
1991
1992
1993
1994
1995
1996
YEAR
INDIA
AUSTRALIA
JAPAN
U.S.A.
FRANCE
GERMANY

FIGURE IX

ANNEXURE 7

TREND IN DEATH RATES PER LAKH PERSONS EMPLOYED IN COAL MINES IN DIFFERENT COUNTRIES

Analysis of Variance Table Unit (PL)^2

Sources of Variation	*D.F.*	*Mean Sqs.*	*F Radio*	*Status of Significance*
Years	9	135.2761		
Countries	5	399.75	2.58184	*
Error	15	154.8314		

Testing the Significance of Arranged Means

India	*Japan*	*USA*	*Germany*	*Australia*	*France*	*CD at 5%*
37.70	31.70	27.30	23.40	22.70	21.30	11.21

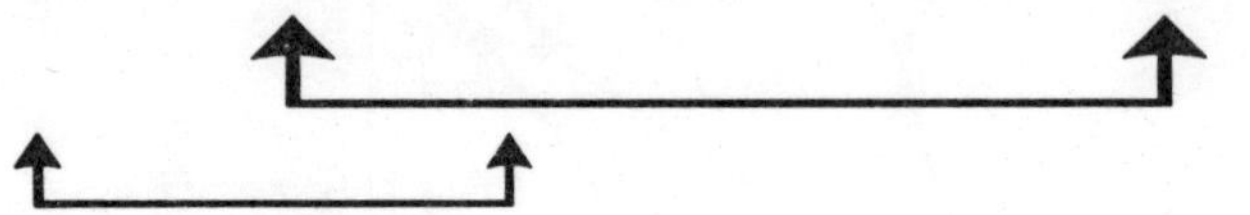

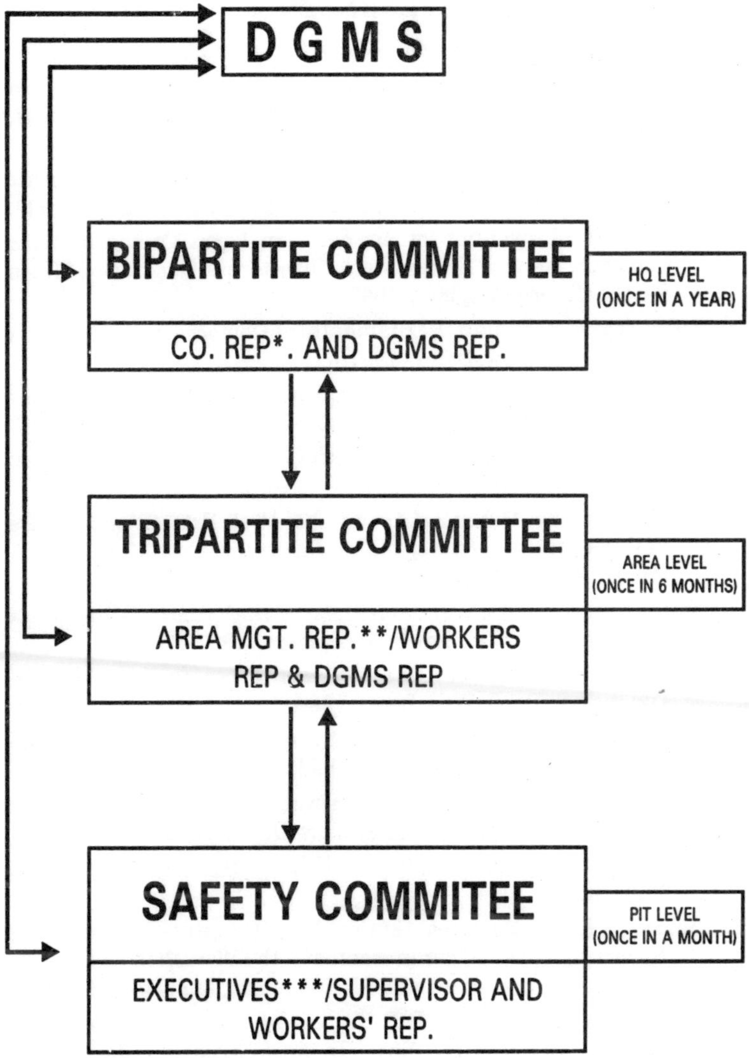

* CMD, All HoD's, ISO Team

** GM, All HoD's and PO's

*** DGMS' Authorised Manager and Safety Officer

Figure X

REFERENCES

Coal Compenium ISSN 0907–0064.

Das, C.R.: Infrastructure Needs of the Coal Industry–in Gondwana, *Journal of Indian Institute of Coal Management*, Ranchi, Vol. 2, No. 1, March, 1997.

Della–Giustina, Daniel E.: *Safety and Environmental Management*, N.Y., Van Nostrand Reinhold Publication, 1996.

Dutta, S.K.: Prevention of Accidents in Open Cast Mines. In Souvenir, Annual Safety Week Directorate General of Mines Safety (Ranchi Region), 1997.

Fifty Years of Indian Parliamentary Democracy, Lok Sabha Secretariat, New Delhi, 1997.

Govt. of India, Ministry of Labour, Directorate General of Mines Safety Annual Reports and Standard Notes.

Heyel, Carl (Ed.): *The Encyclopaedia of Management*: N.Y. Van Nstrand Reinhold Co.

Mahajan, Vinay: Mines Safety in India–Past, Present and Future in Gondwana, *Journal of Indian Institute of Coal Management*, Vol. 2, No. 1, March, 1997.

Molak, Vlasta (Ed.): *Fundamentals of Risk Analysis and Risk Management*, N.Y.: Lewis Publishers, 1997.

Mullen, Samuel: *Emergency Planning Guide for Utilities*, Oklahoma: Penn Well Book, 1994.

Proceeding of the 7th National Symposium on Environment–Indian School of Mines, Dhanbad, 5-7 Feb, 1998.

Report of the Committee on Integrated Coal Policy, Planning Commission, Govt. of India, New Delhi, 1996.

Ridley, John (Ed.): *Safety at Work*, U.K.: Butterworth Heinemann Publication, 1994.

Sarkar, S.K. and Banerjee, G.: Coal Mine Disaster–The Inevitable Recurring Cycle. Paper presented in the Workshop on Disaster Management in Mines and Mining Areas; August 30-31, 1994.

Sharan, R. and Sharma, G.P.: *Impact of Coal Mining on Social Ecology*: A Tentative Note. In *Socio-Economic Impacts of Environment*, (Ed.), B.B. Dhar and N.C. Saxena, New Delhi: Ashish Publishing House, 1993.

Turner, Berry A. and Pidgeon, Nick F.: *Man-made Disaster*: U.K., Butterworth Heinemann Publication, 1997.

10

Disaster Management: A Perspective

SUBHASH SHARMA

The term 'disaster' may be defined as an unexpected happening causing a huge loss of life and property. It may be both natural as well as man-made, in the sense that in some parts of the country, floods are coming due to the construction of checkdams and embankments on the rivers. Disaster may come and ruin the life and property of the people in the forms of earthquakes, cyclones, floods, drought, fire, etc. According to one estimate, about 5,200 disasters took place in 178 countries of the world during 1963-92. Out of these, 787 disasters took place in Asia between 1963 and 1992 causing more than 100 deaths in each case. As discussed earlier major disasters may be defined as those causing at least one of the three consequences which are as follows:

(a) Causing damage to more than 1 per cent of Gross National Product (G.N.P.); or

(b) Affecting more than 1 per cent of total population of an area; or

(c) Causing deaths of more than 100 persons at a time and place.

According to another estimate during 1950-92 about 5 lakh deaths took place out of which 1 per cent in developed countries and 99 per cent in developing countries. Before 1950 the situation was quite different and at that time 30 per cent of total deaths took place in developed countries and 70 per cent in developing countries. These figures indicate the gravity of the situation and seriousness of the problem.

On the basis of time element, earthquakes can be categorized into 3 types— (i) chronic sudden onset, (ii) rare sudden onset and (iii) periodic slow onset. However, intensity and the mitigation measures also play a major role as far as effects of earthquakes are concerned. For instance a very powerful earthquake took place in Guam (West Indies) at 8 point on Richter scale, but no major damages to buildings were caused. On the other hand, on June 12, 1897 an earthquake took place at 8.7 point on Richter scale in Shillong, Meghalaya which resulted into a huge loss of life and property. Not only this, in September 1993 an earthquake took place in Latur (Maharashtra) at 6.3 points only on Richter scale, but it caused deaths of 7611 persons as per government report whereas foreign agencies like World Bank estimated about 9000 deaths. In addition, 19013 houses were fully damaged, 2,45,067 houses were partially damaged, 2,126 cattle died and 1,70,000 persons were affected in total in Latur. Probably considering these huge losses due to disasters, United Nations has declared 1990's as the "International Decade for Natural Disaster Reduction."

All said and done, the point remains as to how to prevent, predict and mitigate major disasters? So far scientific and technological developments have not reached that stage of perfect prediction and prevention of earthquakes and cyclones, though floods, droughts, fires, etc., may be prevented and predicted to some extent, but there is no doubt that a proper planning and effective management can reduce the effects and hazards of disasters, since it is not the earthquake itself but the defective buildings which cause loss of life and property. Though earthquakes occur more often in Japan but their buildings are not falling like a house of cards as happened in Latur. One theory propounds that Indian plate is moving towards Asian plate and hence this collision resulting in earthquakes. Needless to say that Himalayas are the youngest mountains in the world and are still growing. In China, once the behaviour of rats was studied and through peculiar behaviour of rats the Chinese could predict the coming of earthquake but they failed to detect later earthquakes. However, some scientists are still researching on behaviours of birds and animals as a tool to predict the earthquakes. Prof. A.S. Arya, of Structural Engineering Institute, Roorki (U.P.), is a well-known engineer in this field. He supervised the construction of buildings in Latur during rehabilitation. In brief, for mitigation following steps are to be taken:

Steps to be taken for Mitigation of Loss

Firstly there should be vulnerability assessment of buildings, infrastructure, agriculture, industries, etc. As stated earlier, buildings are the most easy target of an earthquake. For construction of earthquake resistance buildings its site, materials used (cement mortar, RCC casting, steel), shape (square, rectangle type), structural design, construction technique (bend, curing, foundation), maintenance, etc., are important aspects. It has been found that C T and L types of houses are more prone to damages than symmetrical– square, rectangular buildings. Further there should be proper foundation in terms of depth and strength and the entrance door should be away from the corner. In addition, the thickness of the wall should not be too much; rather it should be about 25 to 45 cms at the maximum. In Latur the thickness of walls was about 70 cms and cement mortar was not used for wall construction. Further to resist tension, steel and timber should be used as reinforcement, because brick and mud have less capacity of tension resistance. Therefore, bends should be used at plinth, lentel levels as well as vertical stiffeners should be used in the walls, specially in the corners.

From the viewpoint of vulnerability the whole India is categorized into five zones: (a) not prone, (b) less prone, (c) fairly prone, (d) medium prone, and (e) highly prone. Northeast, Himalayas, Jammu and Kashmir and some parts of Gujarat are highly prone areas. Maharashtra is not in highly prone zone but since the occurrence of a devastating earthquake in 1993 in Latur and Usmanabad districts of Maharashtra, there is rethinking of revising these zones.

Secondly, there should be pre-planning of all the available resources, communication facilities, manpower, etc. Experience has shown that before starting the rescue work, administration has to clean the roads and bridges which are badly damaged therefore, not only an inventory of local resources should be prepared but also bypasses and alternative routes should be identified in the plan itself. Since disaster falls under state subject, the State Government is responsible for rescue, relief and rehabilitation. However, at the national level, Ministry of Agriculture, Government of India, is the nodal agency and there is one Crisis Management Committee in which all departments are represented along with Planning Commission. Recently 9th Finance Commission recommended the sharing of relief between the Centre and State on fifty-fifty basis.

Thirdly, there should be an emergency plan for each and every district in which response mechanism should be clearly spelt out. For instance, what is to be done, when to be done, who will do, what and how to get it done through public, NGOs, army or civil administration should be properly clarified, otherwise the natural disaster results in "chaos, anarchy, and destruction" due to confusion confounded. Further there should be clear role-definition for voluntary organizations. These days a new term has been coined–CBO, i.e., Community Based Organization and it is preferred to outsider NGOs. There is ample census data available about *pucca* and *kaccha* houses existing in every district in the country. Further remote sensing can be of tremendous help for mapping of not only resources like land and water but also infrastructure. However, it would be better to have a detailed village to village survey for making a concrete and effective action plan. There should be an attempt to develop a second line of command so that during an extreme emergency of failure of first line of command, the second line should resume the command automatically. This should be clearly defined in the plan itself. During an earthquake in recent past houses of DM and SP of Uttar Kashi District (UP) were also damaged and SP's only son died therein, but second line of command was missing there because their subordinate officers preferred to visit their respective bosses first and foremost. Further there should be networking of NGOs who should do a particular task at a particular village or *muhalls*, otherwise it results into a competition for publicity as well as stealing the show. For instance, during a disaster in Rohtak

(Haryana), there was a barrier put on the road at the entry point and all NGOs were enquired of as to what they want to do for relief and rehabilitation and in accordance with their supply kit they were allotted a particular village. In addition it has come to our knowledge that some foreign agencies sent noodles, etc., as food but since it is not popular among rural people of India it is of no use. During a cyclone in Hyderabad, some NGOs sent blankets for the affected people but in view of the climate of Hyderabad it is not of much use. Thus, NGOs should know the eating and clothing habits of the affected people. District administration should also apprise them whenever and wherever possible.

Fourthly, there should be proper information and public relation system during a disaster, i.e., there should be a temporary camp/counter to tell the people about the loss of life and property and it should also brief the mass media like newspapers, radio, TV regularly, otherwise the mass media will report inflated figures of losses. For example, in Latur print media played an irresponsible role; *The Hindustan Times* reported 25,000 deaths on first day and next day 30,000 deaths! Though the figures reported by the government were only 7,611 deaths and even World Bank report put it to 9000 deaths at the maximum. In addition VVIPs/VIPs should be dissuaded to visit the affected area in the beginning because it causes not only embarrassment to local administration, but also they become liabilities and a lot of resources (human, security, fooding and lodging, etc.) are diverted towards them, thus their photographs and coverage in newspapers, radio and TV are done at people's cost! One more role information system is to play, that rumours should be contradicted/checked and a sense of feeling of cooperation, self-help, fraternity should be inculcated both through mobile and static public information systems. Further, there should be a random assessment after some time of the occurrence since the State Government is supposed to be informed within 24 hours of the occurrence. In Latur, army reached on the spot before the requisition by the district administration which was informed quite late a villager informed thana and the latter to district officials, village chowkidar did not inform in time. Further the whole administration remained in rescue in one village Kilari (which was the epicentre) but they did not reach in time to other villages—hence more losses of lives and properties took place there.

Finally, there should be public education and training before occurrence of any disaster. In Japan, school children are taught as to what they have to do if earthquake comes. Since literacy rate is poor in India, it is better to demonstrate and educate the masses not only through formal education, but also through video cassettes, TV, panchayat sabha, folk dramas, folk songs, etc. In educating the public, it is not only hi-fi technique, but also local techniques, based on long-term experience of the local people, which should be utilized. For instance, Mr Chandi Pd. Bhatt, the Magasasay award winner, says that if a building wall constructed by laying the bricks, with cement, mortar, header, and stretcher, turn by turn, there will be little effect on building during earthquake. Perhaps due to this technique used in Badri Nath temple building it did not collapse in the last earthquake. Further Mr. Chandi Pd. Bhatt also started the Chipko movement not only for fuel preservation and environment protection but also for disaster aversion, because, through experience they had learnt that in 1971 there was a heavy flood in Alaknanda river caused by massive felling of trees resulting in the flowing of water at a very fast speed to the river from the hills, leading to erosion and landslides. Further, there should be rehearsals and mock drills amongst officials and people before the occurrence. During public education and training, it should be openly discussed that development can increase or reduce the disaster but the point is which type of development is adopted. It should be technologically sound and socially acceptable to the people, otherwise the vicious circle of checkdams and embankments which were supposed to prevent the floods will continue to cause flood while their planners and executing agencies are meddling like Nero while Rome was burning!

Unfortunately, Bihar has seen many major earthquakes in Monghyr, Darbhanga, etc., in 1933 and it recurred in North Bihar in 1988. About flood disasters, the less said the better, since every year floods come and ruin human lives and property and we remain insensitive and casual about the seriousness of this problem. The affected people are tired of it and most of them have lost their initiative, struggle and hope. Consequently some of them have slowly and slowly reconciled to it as their destiny and habituated to perceive relief as "third crop", which is sown by nature, fertilized by people's representatives and their accomplices, harvested by the people and shared by petty officials! Hence we are accustomed to firefighting only when the disaster comes in the form of devil, the point, however, is to mitigate, if not prevent, the disasters.

11

Genesis and Management of Anthropogenic and Natural Hazards in Service Industry

Mamta Sinha

Introduction

With a market economy, industrial development and tourism take rapid strides across the globe making inroads in the backward regions of the developing countries. The role of service industry has increased manifold amidst all odds. The present study attempts to embody an account of the genesis and management of the man induced and natural hazards in hotel industry which includes holiday resorts. The two are one of the principle components in service sector and hence transact over varied terrain and diverse cultural and demographic agglomeration.

The concept of hotels and holiday resorts in their modern form is a legacy of industrial revolution with its consequent consumerism which had to start and grow even in under-developed nations, then. With the gradual change in the geo-political scenario the world over and also the ethnological fabric, there was a corresponding change in the framework, and function of the hotels and the degree of hospitality offered. This was an outcome of the fast changing technological attributes, and growing aspirations of human race with respect to hospitality.

All these were not compatible with the diverse social, economical, technological and infrastructural set-up in different parts of the world. As a result the industry faces hazards—both natural, anthropogenic, and can hence be classified into the following three broad categories 1. Man induced or Anthropogenic. 2. Human behavioural and 3. Natural.

Anthropogenic Hazards

The hazards under this category include:

(i) Waste generation, (ii) Contamination of marine water on beaches and contamination of lacustrine water, (iii) Water shortage, (iv) Contaminated sub-surface water, (v) Inadequate supportive infrastructure, and (vi) Induced slope failure on mountainous slopes.

Waste Generation

This is a continuous process through the consumption of eatables and non-eatables which poses sanitation problems for the hotel occupants and also the neighbouring population. The disposal of solid wastes in the nearby fields or stream generates obnoxious gases due to decay and thus affects the quality of air. Its disposal in the stream degrades the water quality and also adds to the general deterioration of river regime. Substantive chunk of solid waste from most hotels contain non-biodegradable plastic and polythene packets and the grave nature of the ill effects of these, on the ecosystem is now a well-established fact. Most hotels do not care to segregate the solid waste into bio-degradable and, non-bio-degradable bags. Depending upon the texture of the surface soil, the solid waste generated could pollute the shallower aquifer.

Contamination of Marine Water on Beaches and Contamination of Lacustrine Water

This causes unhealthy breathing conditions and at times is unfit for bathing when its dissolved oxygen (DO) content falls below 3 and BOD, COD values exceed and a certain optimum level and when oil and grease level exceed a limit of 1 PPM.

The principal cause of such degradation of sea water is

due to oil splits from the ships, discharge of toxic industrial effluents into the sea through estuaries and streams. The waste (both liquid and solid) generated from the hotels located on beaches does cause detrimental impact on the beach ecology.

The urban municipal waste, industrial waste finding way into the lake make the water unfit or undesirable for bathing or for water sports by the residents of hotels located on lake beaches or on lacustrine islands.

Water Shortage

This is a hazard that can be due to anthropogenic or natural factors. The over pumping by deep tubewells located around the hotels and that of the hotels cause lowering of the water table and this can lead to water shortage. The availability of groundwater depends on the climate of the area, type of aquifer, and its hydrological attributes. Hotels located in arid or semi-arid regions are more prone to this problem.

Contaminated Sub-Surface Water

The quality of subsurface water meeting the drinking, cooking, bathing and other needs of the hotels may get polluted by reckless discharge of toxic industrial effluents, urban effluents at improper sites or location of sanitary landfills at inappropriate sites. The undesirable impact on water quality may lead to health hazards and hard water effect on kitchenware, airconditioning plants, boilers, swimming pools, etc.

Inadequate Supportive Infrastructure

This hazard is not faced by hotels located in mega cities which are very well linked by rail, road and air with the rest of the country and consequently with the other parts of the world. Even electric supply is adequate. But in hotels, motels or holiday resorts located in the inferior mountains, or historical sites situated in the underdeveloped parts of the country; the road condition, may be deplorable, modes of communication may be inadequate and unsatisfactory. Shortage of power supply may be yet another problem.

Induced Slope Failure on Mountainous Slope

Slope failure on the upper slopes of the mountains in response to other anthropogenic activities resulting in exceeding the critical value of limiting slope and destabilizing the parameters that govern the slope stability can result in debris slide, landslide and rock slump. These block the approach road to the hotels/tourist resorts or can even damage the same. Removal of vegetal cover in the upper reaches of the mountains also induces slope instability and subsequent slides of various types.

Remedial Measures

Disposal of solid waste in appropriate containers and ensure with local civic authorities of its proper and speedy removal. Care should also be taken that these wastes are not dumped into the river bed or in the sea or lakes. A periodic monitoring of water quality of sea water on the beaches and lakes will ensure the health safety of guests in hotels. A liaison with civic authority or the 'part and horty' or similar organization would help check the deterioration of water quality through proper treatment of sewerage waste before being dumped into the sea and lake and care could be taken by the plying ships to ensure a check of oil spill. A proper and non-wasteful utilization of water will be a step in preventing waste of ground water. If the waste water generated in the hotel is treated and reutilized for the upkeep of garden, aundry and washing, etc., that would be a very prudent approach for the exploitation as well as conservation of water.

Normally, hotels have their own tubewells which tap deep aquifers that generally remain unaffected by contamination of subsurface water through various polluting sources. However, due to normal ageing of pipes, the quality of water may get adversely affected. So a periodic monitoring of water is desirable to ensure adoption of remedial measures.

Power Shortage

This is yet another problem in developing countries and hence heavy duty generators are essential to meet the power shortage. Under this condition, there are frequent breakdowns of supply from the city electric supply undertaking or supply hours are limited. Hence, to ensure an uninterrupted power supply for lifts, airconditioners, gesysers cooking range, refrigeration, etc., there should be standby generators. At this stage, it would be pertinent to advise use of solar panels for heating the water, energy efficient bulbs, condensers, airconditioners, etc.

For hotels located in mountainous terrains, a watch has to be kept on all activities resulting in mountain slope destabilization that ultimately culminate in slides. Concerned agencies have to be approached to adopt suitable geotechnical measures to prevent impending slide.

HUMAN BEHAVIOURAL

Accidents Due to Failure of Lifts

Negligence in the upkeep of lifts have lead to failure of lifts culminating in serious accidents. A sabotage by miscreants or insurgents can also cause accidents in lift failure. Preventive measures include proper check of the mechanical system of the lift by professionals regularly. A vigilant security is a must to mitigate such an accident by insurgents.

Accidents in Swimming Pool

These accidents take place where the depth of swimming pools is less than the stipulated depth. Drowning deaths in swimming pools can take place even due to carelessness by persons bathing in them. Alert security persons who are expert swimmers should be placed at the site to avoid drowning deaths.

Fire

This hazard can break out due to electric short-circuiting, carelessly thrown cigarette buts, gas leakage in kitchens or explosion in gas tanks. At the root of the latter three lies the callousness in the attitude of staff on duty. Vigilant staff is the foremost factor that governs the control of breaking out of fire. A regular check of gas leakage by electronic devices and the personnels engaged in the monitoring work should ensure that devices fitted or utilized to detect gas leakage or electric short circuit function satisfactorily and that there is no malfunctioning in them. Fire fighting devices should be checked periodically for their proper and efficient functioning and that the hotel must engage a few fire fighting trained personnels. Adequate display of signs towards emergency exit doors should be made prominently. At the construction stage of the hotels, minimum use of materials prone to fire damage will be an added advantage in preventive measure.

Food poisoning

All eatables stored in the kitchen–store or kitchen are prone to decay if not stored strictly as per norms or stored for a long time. Also, spray of pesticides other chemicals to eradicate rodants can lead to poisoning of food stuff (cooked and uncooked). Any lapse in storage trade anywhere or by any one is a cause of great concern for the hospitality as it leads to a great loss of reputation.

Natural Hazards

Hospitality centres under discussion normally face one single natural hazard and that is earthquake. For this purpose, right at the construction stage, adequate geotechnical preventive measures should be strictly adopted. The choice of preventive measures is governed by the siesmicity of the area where the hotel is located. A liaison with agencies engaged in earthquake monitoring and management is suggested before construction to decide upon the choice of remedial measures.

Conclusion

A synthesis of the various types of hazards that effect the hospitality industry clearly leads to its categorization into three major groups and hence can help the management to formulate effective and efficient preventive measures through the services of appropriate professionals.

Of the three broad categories of hazards, listed above, the ones under Anthropogenic induced and Human behavioural particularly need a regular and prompt attention and utilization of services of trained professionals to work with their prudent management.

REFERENCE

Narayan, S.: *Indian Anthropology*, Delhi Gyan Publishing House.

12

Disastrous Approach of the Tribal Development

P.C. Oraon

The tribal life few generations ago, was well adjusted, it cannot be said whether it was happy. Today, there is neither adjustment nor happiness in the life pattern of Indian lives. There culture soil have been constantly eroded by the adopting alien lifestyle thus leaving behind their originality, and their socio-economic and educational status, change the social organisation of the tribal society. Social groupings based on behaviour pattern depending on the nature of ancestors, whether actual or fictitious, locality oriented social groupings, etc., are fast fading away. Social institutions like the Oraon, Dhumkuria and Pelerpa, the Morungs of the Aoonagas, the Ghotul of Muria gonds, etc., are going underground or changing radically.

In the eighteenth century in their effort for the consolidation of the Indian empire the Britishers had to come into contact with the Indian tribe thus facing them into their so-called civilized society resulting sporadic movements and revolts launched by tribal communities from time to time. These revolts were directed against the landlords and sometimes against the government also. The foreign rulers, while suppressing there tribal upheavals were clever though to assess potentialities and based upon the theory of "divide and rule" they began segregating the tribal communities from the rest of the Indian population. The tribal leaders were paid pensions and efforts were made to rehabilitate the tribal communities in reserved areas and in this way, they succeeded in segregating the tribal population from the general society.

After the Independence of the country, the architects of the modern India started to think seriously about the development of the tribal societies in India and made a number of welfare schemes. In the first decade and subsequently after the Independence. Thus comes a spurt of activities related with the tribal development and a huge sum is being earmarked in the yearly budget as well as through five-year plans of the centre and through the state also. A special concept of tribal areas as sub-plan area was created and all the tribal dominated area was notified in the Scheduled areas and a special post equivalent to the Chief Secretary rank was created separately for these sub-plan areas and through these, huge sum of money is being pumped in the name of tribal development and general welfare schemes were launched, in a big hurry without proper and authentic planning and in a most haphazard way. Some of these schemes did well, but a good number of schemes failed to yield the desired result, and only the implementing agencies and the business community were able to develop themselves. It can be called the disastrous approach towards the development of tribals.

We can have a glance of different developmental schemes, that were launched in the near past, and further evaluate the scheme one by one. It will show the actual status of the programme and its results. There are number of schemes launched specially for the tribal groups, which are most backward and need special care and programme but it is a fact that most of the schemes miserably failed to fulfil the objectives, but in the process a huge sum of the public exchequer, is being misused or goes invain. The conditions of the Asur, Birjia, Birhor and a number of other primitive tribes is almost the same as it was in the past, but a big sum is already wasted and the primitive tribesmen are just a silent spectator of these so-called developmental activities and in maximum cases, they tried to run away from the places, where these schemes are being forcibly launched.

In the year 1995, Government of India has sanctioned Seventeen Crores (17 Crores) for the upliftment of these primitive tribes, whose total population is only 2,09,247 as per the census of 1991. Apart from this, World Bank has also sanctioned crores of rupees in the name of plateau development named as Bihar Plateau Development Programme in short BPDP.

Other than BPDP a huge amount has also been spent in the name of ITDP (Integrated Tribal Development Programmes), consolidating the Jawahar Rozgar Yojana (JRY), Indira Awas Yojana, Meso project, etc., in it. There are lot of activities in the educational front also involving a huge sum of money. There are Adult Education Schemes and Bihar Education Schemes and Total Literacy Programmes present, under the able guidance of a senior IAS officer. A huge amount is being spent for the purchase and supply of lanterns, Dari, Chalk, etc., and which ultimately landed only in few houses and kerosene oil sold in the blackmarket in maximum cases. A large chunk of money is spent in the name of making educational environment and countless posters and banners were made to educate and make the illiterate, who is unable to read or write understand. Wall postering and wall writing paper ad, were made to for the eradicate of illiteracy and for illiterate these are some of the examples of misuse of government fund in the name of tribal development, without proper planning and farsightedness.

Still the tribal villages are unapproachable, due to the lack of proper road and means of communication, but a huge sum has already been spent in the paper.

There is lack of even basic medical facility in the remote tribal villages, but there is second of huge sum being spent on paper. Further, these activities are breaking the age old system of self-medication, which is timeterted and based on the herbs and plants, locally available, resulting rise of quackery in the absence of trained and educated doctors, who takes salary on paper only.

These are some glaring example of the disastrous approach of the tribal development.

The tribal economy, based on hunting and food gathering, or Jhum cultivation or axe cultivation, settled agriculture is pathetically insufficient it is lagging far behind on rural economy. It is often further distructive, when we take into account the advanced methods of utilising the soil and further, disturbs the age old practice of their own system.

For the last hundred years or so the entire tribal population has been exposed to a number of external influences and stimulating, it has undergone and submitted to a good many cultural, economic and religious impositions. For example, the converted adivasi is a modern man, free from his past, goes to the modern school and colleges and taxes and profession of in choice, what is pathetic that these converted people tend to alienate themselves from their tribes to such extent that they ultimately detribalize themselves. Now, they are isolated lot, became they neither single fully in the general society nor they are absorbed in their tribal society. It leads to a number of socio-psychological problem. It is more in the "Sanswar" tribes, became unlike converted tribal, they cannot live in reverie (day dreaming).

Chotanagpur and Santhal Pargana area of South Bihar presents a most fascinating phenomena. These pre-history and history live side by side. One can find a lot of such example which can be called a disastrous approach. There in Ranchi or in Tata Nagar in Singhbhum district Dhanbad Coalfields in Santhal Parganas, one can find all the phases of social evolution, from the food gathering and hunting stage to the most modern technological leaps in heavy industries like Heavy Industry Corporation (HEC) or the Sky-Scrapen Complex of dibserent coal offices. A landless family's one year child, witnesses the horrible seen of giant coal cutter machine like shovels of big dumpers getting his tiny huts for the mining activities. These tribal setting change into rural and rural motives submerged into urban and urban pattern get transformed into industrial designs. All these have then necessary impact on the life rythm of the tribals. There phenomena is very common in the tribal villages and even in remote intimates of Chotanagpur Plateau.

The vertical tribes man is fast developing into horizontal values and virtues. This is the great shift and consequently the tribal life is full of tension and resolutions.

The dignity and sanctity of tribal lifestyle is at stake due to these disastrous approach of development and the heed of the house is that the sanctity of the tribal values should be maintained not to be submerged in the so-called ultra developmental activities.

Index